MW01681342

THE FAMILY THAT SINGS

THE FAMILY THAT SINGS

Recovering the Joy of Christian Singing

Scott T. Brown

Church & Family Life

Wake Forest, NC

The Family That Sings
Recovering the Joy of Christian Singing

First Printing: March 2026

Strong's numbers refer to James Strong's *The Exhaustive Concordance of the Bible* (New York: Abingdon, 1890).

Church & Family Life
220 South White St., Wake Forest, NC 27587
www.churchandfamilylife.com

ISBN: 978-1-62418-084-2

Book Design by Turley and Sons Design Co.

Printed in the United States of America.

ENDORSEMENTS

"The church desperately needs to recover robust congregational singing, and Scott Brown has given us a thoroughly biblical and deeply practical guide to do just that. Grounded in a rich biblical theology of singing and filled with wisdom from church history, this book casts a compelling vision for why singing matters—not merely as a component of worship, but as a means of grace that teaches, admonishes, and transforms the people of God. Pastors, song leaders, and parents will find here both the theological foundation and the practical encouragement they need to build a culture of vibrant singing in their churches and homes."

—Scott Aniol, PhD, president, G3 Ministries, Professor of Pastoral Theology, Grace Bible Theological Seminary

"*The Family that Sings* is a timely and much-needed call to recover the God-given gift of worship through song. In an age that prefers man-centered entertainment over the worship of God, Scott reminds us that singing is not peripheral but central to the life of God's people. He shows that congregational singing is both command and an act of love from God. I am especially grateful for the vision he casts for the corporate nature of singing: redeemed voices joined as one body, teaching and admonishing one another while displaying the unity of Christ's church. This book helps unwrap the beauty, necessity, and power of lifting our voices together—not as isolated worshipers, but as a gathered people declaring our great God's praise. I believe this is a gracious exhortation for pastors and believers of every age to help reclaim singing as a privilege and powerful instrument for the glory of God."

—Chris Law, pastor at Geneva Lakes Church in Geneva Lakes, Wisconsin

I sing the mighty pow'r of God,
that made the mountains rise,
That spread the flowing seas abroad,
and built the lofty skies.
I sing the wisdom that ordained
the sun to rule the day;
The moon shines full at His command,
and all the stars obey.

I sing the goodness of the Lord,
who filled the earth with food,
Who formed the creatures through the Word,
and then pronounced them good.
Lord, how Thy wonders are displayed,
where'er I turn my eye,
If I survey the ground I tread,
or gaze upon the sky.

There's not a plant or flow'r below,
but makes Thy glories known,
And clouds arise, and tempests blow,
by order from Thy throne;
While all that borrows life from Thee
is ever in Thy care;
And everywhere that we can be,
Thou, God, art present there.

—Isaac Watts, 1715

. . . and they had two hundred
men and women singers.

—Ezra 2:65

Music is indeed the most beautiful of all
Heaven's gifts to humanity.
It is . . . a true friend, refuge, and comforter.

—Pyotr Ilyich Tchaikovsky

The LORD your God in your midst,
The Mighty One, will save;
He will rejoice over you with gladness,
He will quiet you with His love,
He will rejoice over you with singing.

—Zephaniah 3:17

We must not be content with an orthodox view of God, but must ask that He teach us to worship and adore Him.

—J.I. Packer

CONTENTS

ACKNOWLEDGMENTS

I want to thank Chris Law, Wesley Strackbein, Rebekah Sheats, Chelsea Nastase, and my wife Deborah for their helpful feedback and editorial attention. I am indebted to the works of Scott Aniol, Keith Getty, Dan Kreider, and Bob Kauflin, whom I believe have been used of the Lord, not only to revitalize singing in local church life over the past two decades, but also influence me.

I highly recommend their books:

- Scott Aniol—*Musing on God's Music: Forming Hearts of Praise with the Psalms*, *Biblical Foundations of Corporate Worship*, *Worship in Song: A Biblical Approach to Music and Worship*, *Hymns to the Living God*, and *Let the Children Come: Family Worship on Sunday (and the Other Six Days Too)*
- Keith & Kristyn Getty—*Sing! How Worship Transforms Your Life, Family, and Church*, and *The Sing! Hymnal*
- Dan Kreider—*Awake My Soul* and *Keyboard Harmony for Church Musicians*
- Bob Kauflin—*Worship Matters: Leading Others to Encounter the Greatness of God* and *True Worshipers: Seeking What Matters to God*

God is kind to raise up people like this in time of need. In the pages to follow, you will hear echoes of the things they have been saying for a long time. They have been my teachers. I have tried to take what I have learned from them, from the Word of God, and internalize it, and then communicate to the local church where I am a pastor. This book is the result.

INTRODUCTION

THE PROBLEM OF OUR TIMES

Singing Christianly: An Affront to Entertainment Culture

We live in a world in which most people do not sing—instead, they are entertained by singing. They listen. They are passive. Even the church is marked by entertainment-saturated worship.

Perhaps this is why even in churches you often experience poor, pitiful, listless singing. And the men often don't sing at all. The children either refuse to sing, or they mumble their way through, barely moving their lips.

Why? Perhaps it's because we haven't developed a robust doctrine of singing in the church. As a result, pastors and parents have not considered their roles as singing teachers of their children.

People want to be entertained, but God wants His people to be engaged—body, soul, and spirit—because singing engages the whole being. To sing Christianly means to engage the whole being.

Not only the whole being of the individual must be engaged, but also the whole body of the church together, each person doing his part, each member building up the other members of the body in love.

The stakes are high. The world is loud. It's soundtrack is discipling and catechizing our children with its endless noise. But God has given us a wonderful gift—a counter reformation—to muffle the noisy gongs and clanging cymbals. It opens up the sounds of heaven—the music of another kingdom. That gift is singing.

This book is my effort to stand beside you as a "fellow worker for your joy," and for the joy of your children (2 Cor. 1:24). I want to help you build habits, perspectives, and convictions that will make your heart sing—not just today, but for decades to come.

My goal is to increase your joy in our Lord Jesus Christ every step of your journey to heaven.

Scott Brown
Wake Forest, NC
March 2026

CHAPTER 1

ADMIRE GOD'S GIFT OF SINGING

Singing is a wonderful opportunity to admire God's kindness toward us.

This book seeks to cast a vision for admiring the beauty, power, and necessity for singing in the church and the home. My focus is on the delightfully practical ways the Lord teaches us to sing in His Word.

You'll notice this is a book of exhortations. It is a call to action. I am here to encourage you to fill your whole life—your family and your church—with singing.

Each chapter is an appeal to sing like a Christian—the way the Bible teaches us to sing. We often forget why we are singing—and how. We might have sung songs dozens of times, and we may have become disconnected with *why* we sing and *how* we should sing. That is why I have titled each of the chapters in the form of a call to action.

The chapters are written in such a way that a pastor, song leader, father or mother can use them to instruct and encourage those in their charge on how to sing—and how to experience the joys of singing. Each chapter illustrates one practical element for learning how to sing like a Christian. If we are going to sing, then we should know what it looks like to sing Christianly. Here are some singing lessons from heaven.

We Need More than Preaching

Yes, we need preaching and prayer and the Lord's Supper and fellowship. They fuel the fire of awakening in the church. These means of grace are pivotal, but we need more. We need something else that is unique compared to the rest: singing. It is a unique gift come down from heaven.

Martin Luther called music the "governess of the feelings of the human heart."

> *Music is a fair and lovely gift of God which has often wakened and moved me to the joy of preaching.... Music drives away the devil and makes people [happy].... Next after theology I give to music the highest place and the greatest honor. I would not change what little I know of music for something great. Experience proves that next to the Word of God only music deserves to be extolled as the mistress and governess of the feelings of the human heart. We know that to the devils music is distasteful and insufferable. My heart bubbles up and overflows in response to music, which has so often refreshed me and delivered me from dire plagues.*[1]

Admire God's gift of singing.

---

1. Roland Bainton, *Here I Stand: A Life of Martin Luther* (Peabody, MA: Hendrickson Publishers Marketing, 2015), 351-352.

Questions

1. Why should Christians view singing as a special gift from God rather than merely a musical activity?
2. How does singing help shape the thoughts, affections, and spiritual life of God's people?

Recommended Hymn: "All People That on Earth Do Dwell"

CHAPTER 2

UNWRAP THE GIFT OF SINGING

I will sing and give praise, even with my glory.
Awake, lute and harp!
I will awaken the dawn.
I will praise You, O Lord, among the peoples,
And I will sing praises to You among the nations.
For Your mercy is great above the heavens,
And Your truth reaches to the clouds. —Ps. 108:1-4

Singing is a wonderful gift. When you unwrap it, you discover more than the wrapping on the box reveals. And it is the gift that keeps on giving. You find there are multiple lifegiving treasures within it—for you and for many others. Just as God gave treasures in nature, light, sound, wind, color, food, and water, so He gave us the gift of singing. In singing, God gathers us, lifts us, teaches us, and refines us. God gave birds the gift of singing, and they sing throughout the day. It is beautiful. We should do the same.

Singing is one way God cares for souls. It is a means of gospel proclamation, personal strengthening, and church building. It is a critical part of raising children and strengthening churches. God designed singing to carry you and your church through all the seasons of life.

This is why churches and families—and children—should excel in singing.

And they should be careful with what they sing. Pastors must be careful with music. This is soul-work. It's law and gospel. It's shepherding. It's pastoral care set to melody.

One of my favorite sounds—one of the truly beautiful sounds—is the sound of congregational singing. Singing is an expression of God's love. It is a gift.

We could make a long list of the ways God expresses love to His children. When He said, "I will never leave you nor forsake you," and when He declared, "I will strengthen you, yes, I will help you, I will uphold you with My righteous right hand," He was referring to the many ways He stretches out His hands to His children (Heb. 13:5; Isa. 41:10). When David said, "The Lord is my shepherd; I shall not want," he was referring to the many ways God guides His people (Ps. 23:1). When Jesus said, "I will not leave you orphans," He was summarizing His unbroken care for His children (John 14:18). Singing is one element of that unbroken care.

Singing is but one expression of the multitude of His mercies (Ps. 51:1). Through singing, God mercifully directs our minds, shapes our dispositions, and transforms feelings. Singing carries us to green pastures and quiet waters.

> *"My kindness shall not depart from you," . . . says the Lord, who has mercy on you. (Isa. 54:10)*

Luther said it this way:

I most heartily desire that music, that divine and most precious gift, be praised and extolled before all people.[1]

Singing is a wonderful gift to help us pursue "the chief end of man—to glorify God, and to enjoy him forever."[2]

This is why singing together is just another one of those practices God gave us to keep us close to Him.

For I am persuaded that neither death nor life, nor angels nor principalities nor powers, nor things present nor things to come, nor height nor depth, nor any other created thing, shall be able to separate us from the love of God which is in Christ Jesus our Lord. (Rom. 8:38-39)

Singing connects us with God. This is why singing is such a powerful gift. God makes it a requirement for local church life. This is why it is important that church leaders unwrap the gift and show its many facets to their congregations. Church leaders should take steps to create a culture of vibrant singing. They should mobilize themselves to help the congregation open that gift and experience its many blessings.

Unwrap the gift of singing!

Questions

1. What is God's purpose for us in singing?
2. What gifts does He bestow through singing?

Recommended Hymn: "Come, Thou Fount of Every Blessing"

---

1. Walter E. Buszin and Martin Luther, "Luther on Music," *The Musical Quarterly* 32, no. 1 (January 1946), 81.
2. Westminster Shorter Catechism, Q. 1.

CHAPTER 3

SING WITH GOD'S CREATION!

The universe began with a song, not a bang (Job 38:4-7). Singing is built into the fabric of heaven and earth for all eternity—from eternity past to eternity future. In other words, singing is a big deal to God. It is embedded in the fabric of the universe.

Let's start with a brief flyover of this unfolding, ever soaring, grand scheme of singing in the Bible. You could call this a short "biblical theology." It begins at creation in the heavens, drops down to earthlings, and continues to the new creation in heaven.

We first encounter singing at creation. This is the first declaration of its significance. The first song of the universe appears in Job 38:4-7: "Where were you when I laid the foundation of the earth? . . . when the morning stars sang together, and all the sons of God shouted for joy?"

In these verses, God reveals to Job the scene that occurred at creation before mankind was made. Job is informed that singing is woven into the fabric of the cosmos. Before humans sang, others were singing (either the stars or the angels, depending on how you interpret this verse; there is some evidence that the stars actually broadcast a harmonious sound). Singing begins in heaven and is thrown to earth.

The first actual singing on earth is implied in the creation of musical instruments in Genesis 4:21, where Jubal is mentioned, "the father of all those who play the harp and flute."

The Scriptures are replete with songs and singing:

The first written song in the Bible is recorded in Exodus 15:1-18. This is the song of Moses—a spectacular song of deliverance.

In Exodus 15:20-21, Miriam leads the women of Israel in singing.

In Deuteronomy 31:19-32:43, God commands Moses to write a song and teach it to Israel on the last day of his life—a song to help them remember the works of God.

In Judges 5, we read the words of the song of Deborah and Barak which was sung after the victory over Sisera.

In the Davidic era, we find a flourishing of singing. From 1 Samuel through 2 Chronicles, there is an explosion of references to singing.

In 1 Chronicles 6:31-32, David deploys Levites to minister with music.

In 1 Chronicles 15 and 16, singing is formalized in temple worship.

The Psalms are composed of 150 songs for every category of human experience including, worship, lament, thanksgiving, joy, praise, wisdom, and war. God has given us 150 tracks for every station of the soul.

The prophets were singers who wrote songs:

Isaiah wrote several songs (Isa. 5, 12, 35, 42).

Jeremiah sings of the new covenant, and even the structure of Lamentations reflects the poetic elements of singing (Jer. 31:12; Lam. 5:14).

After the exile, we find that singing accompanies the rebuilding of the temple. This singing includes choirs and instruments (Ezra 3:10-11; Neh. 12:27-47).

The New Testament reflects another explosion of singing beginning with the announcement of the Messiah:

- Mary's Magnificat (Luke 1:46-55)
- Zechariah's song (Luke 1:68-79)
- The singing of the angels (Luke 2:14)
- Simeon's song (Luke 2:29-32)

Jesus and the disciples sang a hymn after the Last Supper before they departed to the Mount of Olives (Matt. 26:30; Mark 14:26). This song was probably the Hallel, recorded in Psalms 113-118.

In Acts, Paul and Silas sang in prison (Acts 16:25).

In Romans 15:9, Christ identifies Himself as the global worship leader after the pattern of David, singing a psalm of thanksgiving which quotes Psalm 18:49.

The Corinthian church is taught to sing with the spirit and the mind (1 Cor. 14:15).

In his other letters, Paul teaches the Ephesian and Colossian churches how to sing (Eph. 5:18-20; Col. 3:16).

In Hebrews, Jesus is singing with the congregation (Heb. 2:12, quoting Ps. 22:22-25):

I will declare Your name to My brethren;
In the midst of the assembly I will praise You.
You who fear the LORD, praise Him!
All you descendants of Jacob, glorify Him,

And fear Him, all you offspring of Israel!
For He has not despised nor abhorred the affliction of
the afflicted;
Nor has He hidden His face from Him;
But when He cried to Him, He heard.
My praise shall be of You in the great assembly;
I will pay My vows before those who fear Him.

At the marriage supper of the Lamb, the redeemed sing "Hallelujah" (Rev. 19:1-8).

In Revelation, singing continues in heaven—multitudes upon multitudes of singers (Rev. 5:9-10; 14:3; 15:3-4).

In short, singing is a signature activity in God's kingdom. Creation was celebrated in song by the angels, and the people of God are singing throughout history. Finally, millions of the redeemed in heaven are singing with unquenchable joy. Singing is embedded in the cosmos.

Not all believers can sing like opera stars, but they can sing along with God the Father, the Lord Jesus, and the gathered saints. And they can sing out of love—for without love, singing is only a noisy gong and a clanging cymbal (1 Cor. 13:1).

Sing with God's creation!

Questions

1. What is the first recorded instance of singing in God's creation?
2. What are some of the examples of singing we see throughout Scripture?

Recommended Hymn: "O for a Thousand Tongues to Sing"

CHAPTER 4

SING FOR REVIVAL

Singing has played an important role in revivals. During the Great Awakening (1730s-40s), George Whitfield, Jonathan Edwards, John and Charles Wesley, and others wrote, curated, and sang hymns of worship in earnest. Six thousand songs were written by Charles Wesley alone. Isaac Watts and others of his generation penned some of the most widely sung hymns. Many of these hymns are still sung today: "When I Survey the Wondrous Cross," "Jesus Shall Reign," "O for a Thousand Tongues to Sing," and "And Can It Be?"

Jonathan Edwards wrote of the change that occurred in corporate singing during these revivals:

> *Our public* praises *were then greatly enlivened; God was then served in our* psalmody, *in some measure in the* beauty of holiness. . . . *there has been scarcely* any part *of divine worship, wherein good men amongst us have had* grace so drawn forth, *and their hearts so lifted up, as in* singing *his praises.*[1]

1. Jonathan Edwards, "A Faithful Narrative of the Surprising Work of God in the Conversion of Many Hundred Souls in Northampton," in Edward Hickman, ed., *The Works of Jonathan Edwards*, A.M., Vol. 1 (London: Ball, Arnold, and Company, 1840), 348.

In the Welsh Revival of 1904–05, there was a similar outpouring of praise. These hymns, among others, caught fire at the time: "Here Is Love, Vast as the Ocean" and "Jesus, Lover of My Soul."

The singing during the Welsh Revival was not only beautiful and electrifying; it was sanctifying. It forged unity, brought conviction, fomented healing, and spawned joy. People who had never sung before lifted their voices in praise. Communities were changed—not just by sermons but by the power of singing. People began singing in pubs and workplaces. In mining communities, workers returning from a revival meeting would walk through the streets singing hymns. This was so common that newspapers wrote about it.[2]

Matthew Henry captured the reviving nature of singing in his exposition of Psalm 150:1:

> *Praise ye the Lord. Praise God with a strong faith; praise him with holy love and delight; praise him with an entire confidence in Christ; praise him with a believing triumph over the powers of darkness; praise him with an earnest desire towards him, and a full satisfaction in him; praise him by a universal respect to all his commands; praise him by a cheerful submission to all his disposals; praise him by rejoicing in his love, and solacing yourselves in his great goodness; praise him by promoting the interests of*

2. Digby L. James, ed., *The Religious Revival in Wales: Contemporaneous Newspaper Accounts of the Welsh Revival of 1904–05* (Weston Rhyn: Quinta Press, 2004).

> *the kingdom of his grace; praise him by a lively hope and expectation of the kingdom of his glory.*[3]

Robust singing is often a sign of revival.

Thankfully, the church in the 21st century is experiencing a revival of congregational singing. Not just singing, but theologically driven singing. Not just theological singing but beautiful singing. There is a revival of psalm singing, and there are writers of new songs. These writers are inspiring a new generation of singers in the church. They are teaching the church afresh how to sing. I hope this uprising of singing is a sign of an even greater revival.

Sing for revival!

Questions

1. Why do you think revivals are often marked by singing?
2. Do you think passionate singing is always a sign of true revival?

Recommended Hymn: "Revive Us Again"

3. Matthew Henry, *Commentary on the Whole Bible* (1706–1710), on Psalm 150:1.

CHAPTER 5

SING AS AN ACT OF LOVE

I love you, O Lord, my strength. —Ps. 18:1

I beseech you therefore, brethren, by the mercies of God, that you present your bodies a living sacrifice, holy, acceptable to God, which is your reasonable service. —Rom. 12:1

Love is the beginning of singing. This is why singing is an act of love. The *impulse* of the singing soul is love, and the *impact* of the singing soul is cultivation of a loving soul. It is an act of love for God. The believer presents his body "a living sacrifice, acceptable to God," which is the way he worships the Lord. We worship out of love. God created singing to demonstrate our love for Him, for our own souls, for our brethren, and for the unbeliever.

Augustine said this: "It is not the voice but the desire that God hears; not the musical string but the sounding heart."[1]

The Holy Spirit—the Spirit of love—is like the breath in a wind instrument. The God-breathed Word, activated by the

1. Augustine, *Expositions on the Psalms 73–98*, trans. Maria Boulding, *The Works of Saint Augustine*, III/18 (Hyde Park, NY: New City Press, 2002), Exposition on Psalm 85:1.

Spirit, fills our minds and produces the music. Even the finest woodwind instrument is useless without breath. Without this, it can't produce a sound. Ephesians 5:18 calls us to be filled with the Spirit so that we can sing spiritual songs—not just with our mouths, but with hearts stirred by divine wind (John 3:8).

David said: "Awake, my glory; awake, harp and lyre!" (Ps. 57:8). A clock won't run unless the weights are lifted. In the same way, our spirits must be awakened and lifted to properly worship God. How does this happen? The Spirit of God does it. We are told to pray in the Spirit, and we must sing in the Spirit too (1 Cor. 14:15-16; Jude 20).

Singing without loving is just meaningless buzzing. It is "sounding brass or a clanging cymbal" (1 Cor. 13:1). Without love, we become instruments of noise instead of vessels of praise. There's still sound in our singing, but it's just noise.

The heart must be in harmony with the voice, or the entire instrument of worship is off-key. Singing is designed in such a way that the strings of your mind, body, and soul are all vibrating together. This puts your body in harmony with heaven.

Therefore if we would improve our singing, we must first fan the flames of our love for God and His kingdom. The love comes first in the same way that Jesus told us: "If you love Me, [you will] keep my commandments" (John 14:15).

Sing as an act of love.

Questions

1. Without love, what is singing like?
2. How does singing cultivate love for a lifetime?

Recommended Hymn: "Jesus, Lover of My Soul"

CHAPTER 6

SING BECAUSE YOU MUST

Sing, O daughter of Zion!
Shout, O Israel!
Be glad and rejoice with all your heart,
O daughter of Jerusalem! –Zeph. 3:14

Singing is not *only* an impulse of love and a cultivation of love; it is also an act of obedience. Why do we sing in church? Why do we sing in our families? We sing because God commands us to sing. We are under orders. This is what Christians do. To refuse to sing as a Christian is to defy God.

As Keith and Kristyn Getty state, "Not to sing is to disobey."[1]

Carl Trueman wrote: "We Protestants boast of being people of the book. To be fully Protestant, we need also to be people of song."[2]

God has commanded His people to be a singing family. In fact, there are over 50 direct commands and over 400

1. Keith and Kristyn Getty, *Sing! How Worship Transforms Your Life, Family, and Church* (Brentwood, TN: B&H Publishing Group, 2017), 13.
2. Carl Trueman, *The Rise and Triumph of the Modern Self: Cultural Amnesia, Expressive Individualism, and the Road to Sexual Revolution* (Wheaton, IL: Crossway, 2020), 423.

references to blessing the Lord through singing in Scripture.[3] Compare this with the commands to pray (250-300) or to give thanks (150+) or to fear God (300). It has been estimated that 25 percent of these singing commands are focused on individual singing, and the rest refer to corporate gatherings.

God prioritizes corporate singing as a means of sanctifying His people. Singing is a critical element in accomplishing this. Thus singing is one important sign that a church is striving to be faithful to the Lord and to edify His people. Bluntly: a Christian who is able to sing and does not sing is a disobedient Christian.

Singing is simply a matter of "the regulative principle of worship." This principle argues that when it comes to the worship of God, the church must do what the Scriptures require. It is based on the proposition that only God is authorized to design worship. Moses describes it in this way:

> *You shall not worship the* L*ORD your God in that way; . . . Whatever I command you, be careful to observe it; you shall not add to it nor take away from it (Deut. 12:31-32).*

God must be worshiped the way He wants to be worshiped. And in the Scriptures God requires the church to sing. It is something we must do. A biblical church must also be a singing church.

This is communicated in chapter 22 of the London Baptist Confession of 1689. Paragraph 5 identifies the elements of biblically ordered worship. They are:

---

3. Bob Kauflin, "Words of Wonder: What Happens When We Sing?" Desiring God 2008 National Conference, September 27, 2008. https://www.desiringgod.org/messages/words-of-wonder-what-happens-when-we-sing. Accessed July 13, 2025.

> *The reading of the Scriptures, preaching, and hearing the Word of God, teaching and admonishing one another in psalms, hymns, and spiritual songs, singing with grace in our hearts to the Lord; as also the administration of baptism and the Lord's supper, are all parts of religious worship of God, to be performed in obedience to him, with understanding, faith, reverence, and godly fear.*[4]

We do not sing merely because we like it or have musical talent. If that were the case, many people would abstain from singing due to their ineptitude.

We don't sing because it is a good thing to do or because we like the tunes, or to be countercultural. Rather, we sing because we believe that the Scripture is sufficient. God tells us *to* sing, *what* to sing, *why* we should sing, *whom* we should to sing to, *where* to sing, and also *how* to sing.

The Scriptures are filled with numerous commands to sing. Here are two examples among many:

In Psalm 96:1-2 we are told:

> *Oh, sing to the LORD a new song!*
> *Sing to the LORD, all the earth.*
> *Sing to the LORD, bless His name;*
> *Proclaim the good news of His salvation*
> *from day to day.*

A similar command is issued in Psalm 47:6-7:

> *Sing praises to God, sing praises!*
> *Sing praises to our King, sing praises!*
> *For God is the King of all the earth;*
> *Sing praises with understanding.*

---

4. 1689 London Baptist Confession of Faith, 22.5.

It is important to obey these commands because we need to be transported to better pastures. Singing takes us into territory that we might not arrive at on our own. God wants to pull us out of ourselves and into Him.

When you sing, you are doing what God has commanded you to do (Col. 3:16; Eph. 5:18-19). God desires us to sing as an obedient church.

Sing because you must!

Questions

1. What should I do if I don't think I'm a very good singer?
2. What are the reasons why I should sing to overcome my reluctance?

Recommended Hymn: "Praise to the Lord, the Almighty"

CHAPTER 7

SING TO HARMONIZE THE CHURCH

Singing unifies a church. When we sing as a congregation, we sing together off the same page. We say the same words. We declare the same truth. We sing the same tune. In doing so, we are blended together in unity. We are not doing our own thing; we are doing what everyone else is doing. We are harmonizing the church.

Jonathan Edwards states: "The best most perfect way that we have of expressing a sweet concord of mind to each other is by music."[1]

Think of a symphony orchestra with dozens of instruments playing together—strings, bass, woodwinds, percussion—all different yet all in harmony. The church brings different voices and preferences and personalities together to sing the same "score."

1. Thomas A. Schafer, ed., *The Works of Jonathan Edwards, The "Miscellanies,"* a-500 (New Haven, CT: Yale University Press, 1994), Miscellanies 188. Cited in Keith & Kristyn Getty, *Sing!*

- Singing is a social experience.
- We are sharing the sounds.
- We are unified in the message of the song.
- It creates a sense of community.
- It gives a church shared sounds.
- It unifies us with shared language.
- It binds us together in shared doctrine.
- It gives us shared emotions.

In a beehive, thousands of bees work together in perfect rhythm. Each bee has a role. Their vibration, their buzzing, is shared language.

Here's another illustration: an orchestra. The sound of an orchestra can have a profound impact on the human body. It can alter heartrate, breathing, endorphin release, and even muscle tension. The sounds can increase adrenaline levels and promote relaxation. They can stimulate a wide range of emotions. Research supports the idea that during live musical performances, especially at classical concerts, the heartbeats of the audience can synchronize. Music can align physiological and emotional responses among the participants—even to the heartbeat.[2]

But participants also receive profound encouragement in singing. Singing teaches us that we are not alone. We have each other as brothers and sisters in the family of Christ. We hear other voices surrounding us. And we experience what is pictured in the first three chapters of Revelation—that Christ

2. Eric W. Dolan, "Scientists observe a remarkable synchronization effect among classical music listeners," PsyPost, August 24, 2024, https://www.psypost.org/scientists-observe-a-remarkable-synchronization-effect-among-classical-music-listeners/. Accessed March 12, 2026.

Himself is walking among the lampstands of His church. What is He doing? He is singing with us.

Generational Unity

Multigenerational worship is the biblical pattern. Ephesians 5:18-21 affirms this. The Apostle Paul assumes that children and the whole range of ages are together in the meeting of the church. This is why it is important that we have unity across the generations in our worship. God intends singing to unite the generations. Is it possible that the Devil has sought to use musical genres to divide the church?

Our culture prioritizes and worships youth. This has had an enormous impact on church singing. Some churches focus on catering their music to the youth alone rather than all ages.

In contrast, an important characteristic of congregational singing is that it engages the whole family, from the youngest to the oldest. As Isaac Watts aptly declares in his great 1719 hymn "Jesus Shall Reign,"

People and realms from every tongue
Dwell on His love with sweetest song;
And infant voices shall proclaim
Their early blessings on His name.

Singing helps us do this. The young and old are together, singing off the same page. Music is meant to be one of the places where all generations intersect and connect as one body.

This will probably look differently in different churches. In my home church, singing incorporates songs, both old and new. In our song selections, we seek to use the best of yesterday and today. We are comfortable singing songs which draw from hymnology dating back to the 18th century as well as contemporary pieces composed in the modern era. Neither do we think that "old is good; new is bad" or that "new is good; old is bad."

Finally, there is probably no way for everyone to come into a local church and appreciate every genre of music we sing. We all have a different background. We have diverse musical tastes. It is easy to love one genre and hate another, so be humble. Be submissive to the leaders of the church as they seek to bring people together as a unified body. Whether church members are young or old, refined or unrefined, great singers or poor singers—according to Scripture, all can be *great* singers.

Like an ocean, every wave is made up of millions of drops of water, all moving together to the shore. No single drop defines the whole, just like the ocean of voices in the church mingling into a wave to move God's people together in unity.

Sing to harmonize the church.

Questions

1. How does singing bring harmony to a church? List the ways.
2. Why is generational unity and continuity important, and how does singing foster it?

Recommended Hymn: "Blest Be the Tie that Binds"

CHAPTER 8

SAVOR THE SOUND OF VOICES

A Psalm of David.
I will sing of mercy and justice;
To You, O Lord, I will sing praises. —Ps. 101:1

Let the word of Christ dwell in you richly in all wisdom, teaching and admonishing one another in psalms and hymns and spiritual songs, singing with grace in your hearts to the Lord. —Col. 3:16

If a church could be compared to a sound, what would the sound be? It's the sound of voices![1]

The sounds of mingled human voices singing in the church is a treasure—in audio. There are many beautiful sounds the Lord has given humanity to enjoy. Listen to the sounds of birds singing. Hear the wind blowing through the leaves of trees, a river flowing, waves breaking, ice cracking on a lake in the dead of winter. These are all wonderful sounds.

1. Keith and Kristyn Getty, *Sing! How Worship Transforms Your Life, Family, and Church* (Nashville: B&H Publishing Group, 2017), 15.

But what is the defining sound in a church of Jesus Christ? Clearly, it is the sound of God's people lifting their voices. When David said "blessed are the people who know the joyful sound," he began that psalm by proclaiming that he was singing to the Lord. His "joyful sound" was referring to the sounds of singing in the worship of God (Ps. 89:15).

The church is almost the only place in our culture where people sing together. Singing doesn't typically happen at a play, a movie theater, a restaurant, a store, or a civic meeting. The church stands out among the institutions of the world. It is a glaring difference. She sings. She sings because God has clearly commanded her in His Word to sing.

In John Stott's *The Cross of Christ,* W. M. Clow writes:

> *A Buddhist temple never resounds with a cry of praise. Mohammedan worshippers never sing. . . . [Their prayers] are never jubilant with the songs of the forgiven.*[2]

What then does the Bible require? It requires singing. Within the New Testament, Paul tells two churches to exercise their human voices (Eph. 5:17-19; Col. 3:12-17). Every one of the psalms in the Old Testament confirm this.

In our church, we try to prioritize the sound of the voices. We use instruments, but we don't want the instruments to overwhelm the voices. Neither do we want the song leader's voice to dominate the voices of the congregation. It is a delicate balance.

One of the maladies of modern church singing is that it is often centered on the loudness of the band, not the voices of the congregation. When my kids have visited megachurches,

---

2. John R. W. Stott, *The Cross of Christ* (Downers Grove, IL: IVP Books, 2006), 251.

they tell me it's so loud that the ushers sometimes pass out ear plugs.

I once visited a church in which, if the band's sound system had been turned off, I would have heard nothing. The people were not singing. They were being entertained. The band was great, but the people were dull. The focus was on the musicians on stage. The congregation was being entertained by great singers and a band rather than singing themselves. This environment curates spectators, not participants—watchers, not worshipers.

Here is my view: the sound of voices, not loud instruments, should command the central place in the music of the church. Let the congregation hear the beauty of the voices in one accord. In Psalm 66:2, David puts it this way: "Sing out the honor of His name; make His praise glorious."

Singing is a social experience. When we sing together, we are sharing the sounds of worship through melodic words and the messaging of the music. Singing unifies the church. It creates a sense of community. It gives a church shared sounds, shared language, and shared emotions—shared doctrine. In other words, Christ builds His church not only with hammers but also with harmonies.

Savor the sound of voices.

Questions

1. Why are voices such a treasure in congregational worship?
2. What's the problem with overly loud musical instruments in a worship service?

Recommended Hymn: "All Creatures of Our God and King"

CHAPTER 9

SING BECAUSE GOD MADE YOU LIKE A MUSICAL INSTRUMENT

The first musical instrument God created was the human body. You were made to sing. Yes, your body is a musical instrument. As Robert S. Smith puts it: "song is of the body, by the body, for the whole body of Christ."[1]

Let this sink in: the original and first instrument that God created was the human body. More instruments were created later (Gen. 4:21-22), but the body came first.

Singing engages your whole being—physical, mental, and spiritual. It includes:

- Raising the voice (Ps. 100:1-5)
- Shouting (Zeph. 3:14)
- Clapping of hands (Ps. 47:1)
- Lifting of hands (Ps. 63:4; 134:2)

1. Robert S. Smith, "Hymnopolis: Song, City and Citizenship." *Themelios* 45, no. 2 (August 2020), 267-283.

- Spreading out of hands (Ps. 88:9)
- Kneeling (2 Chron. 6:12-13)
- Bowing down (Ps. 95:6)

Singing is not spiritually disconnected from the body. It is not ethereal. It is not simply spiritual and pietistic. It is physical—embodied!

Even the Hebrew word for "worship" implies bodily engagement. It means *to bow down.*[2] The Levites stood to thank and praise the Lord (1 Chron. 23:30). Paul tells us to present our whole bodies as living sacrifices (Rom. 12:1-2). Singing is spirituality translated into physicality.

Here are some of the elements of embodied worship:

Voice

Consider the simplest part of your musical instrument—your voice. The Bible describes singing as raising your voice. Your vocal cords are like strings on a guitar. They vibrate and produce sounds when you talk and when you sing. Yes, God gave you vocal muscles that operate like strings in your throat—like a violin, one of the most expressive instruments ever created.

Resonance Chambers

Your throat, mouth, and nasal cavities are like resonance chambers—like the body of a guitar, which is a sound chamber. It transmits vibration and frequency. By changing the shape of those air openings and closings of the mouth

2. Strong's H7812: שָׁחָה (shâchâh), bow down. Definition from Francis Brown, S. R. Driver, and Charles A. Briggs, *A Hebrew and English Lexicon of the Old Testament* (Oxford: Clarendon Press, 1907).

and the operation of the trachea, lungs, diaphragm, rib cage, and breathing muscles, you alter the tone. Your lips, tongue, and teeth also articulate sounds in the same way as a flutist's fingers or a violinist's bow change notes. Your vocal cords and your resonance chambers can produce various forms of falsetto, whispering, or simply belting it out.

Diversity

No voices are the same. Every person has a particular range and depth to their voice. Some are high pitched, others low. These voice patterns have formal classifications, such as bass, basso profundo, bass-baritone, baritone, lyric baritone, dramatic baritone, tenor, lyric tenor, spinto tenor, dramatic tenor, countertenor, contralto, mezzo-soprano, lyric mezzo-soprano, dramatic mezzo-soprano, coloratura soprano, lyric soprano, spinto soprano, and dramatic soprano. God has given each of us a unique voice to use as we join together in praising Him.

But I Can't Sing!

Unless you are mute, you cannot reasonably say, "I can't sing." Rather say: "I can't sing as well as I wish I could." Many of these orchestral body functions can be improved and even changed with practice. That's why we ought not say, "I can't sing." Take steps to improve your current skill. Say: "God made me an instrument, and I can improve my vocal skills just like most skills can be improved." Say: "It's okay; I don't need to be a soloist to play my instrument."

So, if you say, "I can't sing" and yet God has commanded you to sing, what of it? Will you use that excuse for other commands of God? Can a husband say, "I'm not good at serving," or "I'm not good at showing mercy," or "I'm not naturally good at loving my wife"? Or can a child say, "Obeying my parents isn't easy for me, so I'm okay with where I am"? Absolutely not. Just because something doesn't come as naturally to me as to others doesn't give me a pass before God to disobey His command.

The world is full of people who don't sing because they've never taken the time to learn. Your voice can improve with breathing exercises, practicing various singing functions like pitch glides, humming, vocal scales, and consonant exercises. Posture also makes a difference. Like any muscle, regular, consistent practice can improve vocal strength and precision.

As you can see, the body is not simply an instrument; it is an entire orchestra.

If someone asks you if you play an instrument, say: "Yes! My body is my musical instrument. I play it every day. I play it at home, in the car, and in church every week."

And if you would like to exercise and improve the sound of your voice, these resources might be helpful: *Cantabile: A Manual about Beautiful Singing for Singers, Teachers of Singing and Choral Conductors* by Katharin Rundus, and *Building Beautiful Voices* by Paul Nesheim.

Yes, it is possible to improve your singing skills! So what's the harm in learning to sing better? Master your instrument.

Sing because God made you like a musical instrument!

Questions

1. What was the first musical instrument ever created?
2. Name the various parts of your body that are used when you sing.

Recommended Hymn: "Trust and Obey"

CHAPTER 10

SING, YOU MEN

Men are the spiritual marines in the church. They are specifically designed to be leaders and conquerors. This should be evident in their singing.

Modern feminism and masculine effeminacy have gutted manly singing in the church. The songs are soft, breathy, and drained of strength. They are more like emotional love songs you would sing to your wife. I've heard them referred to as "Jesus is my girlfriend" songs. Where is the strength? Where is the manly valor? Where is the victory? It's no wonder the men are silent!

One of the most powerful things to experience in a church is to hear manly voices blasting away. It makes sense. Many of our hymns are powerful statements of the majesty and omnipotent power of God or the boast of victory in war.

But in the modern church, men often don't sing. Yet the Scriptures give us numerous instances of men singing.

Moses, David, and Isaiah all sang (Exod. 15:1; Ps. 23, etc; Isa. 5:1-7).

In the New Testament, not only is the whole church commanded to sing, but men are found singing in small groups as well. The disciples sang in the upper room (Matt. 26:30). Paul and Silas sang in prison (Acts 16:25).

> *But at midnight Paul and Silas were praying and singing hymns to God, and the prisoners were listening to them (Acts 16:25).*

In the Bible, men sing (2 Chron. 5:13; Ps. 68:25; Ezra 3:10-11)!

I've known men who intentionally show up late for church so they miss the singing; they just want to hear the sermon. However, I don't completely blame them. With the effeminacy of so many songs, I can understand why they'd rather not take part!

Men don't respond very well to that kind of singing.

In our present historic moment, many modern worship songs are on the soft side. It's a trend. There are more breathy songs than ever. Many of the most popular worship songs are sung by beautiful women—not men.

A number of years ago, an article appeared with this direct title: "Men want 'macho' hymns, fewer flowers and less dancing in church."[1] The message: Men want strong songs that declare truth. They would rather not sing songs that are too emotional or "too girly."

> *The survey found men would rather sing passionate hymns such as Amazing Grace, rather than 'sentimental, lovely dovey songs.' . . .*
>
> *Nearly 60 percent of those who took part in a survey said they enjoyed singing—but added*

1. Daily Mail Reporter, "Men want 'macho' hymns, fewer flowers and less dancing in church," *Daily Mail*, May 5, 2009, https://www.dailymail.co.uk/news/article-1177585/Men-want-macho-hymns-fewer-flowers-dancing-church.html. Accessed July 15, 2025.

> *comments showing they preferred anthemic songs and 'proclamational' hymns as opposed to more emotional love songs.*

The article suggested a top 10 list of "male-friendly hymns":

- Onward Christian Soldiers
- And Can It Be
- Guide Me, O Thy Great Redeemer
- All People That on Earth Do Dwell
- Be Thou My Vision
- How Great Thou Art
- Amazing Grace
- Eternal Father, Strong to Save (For Those in Peril on the Sea)
- Our God Reigns
- Dear Lord and Father of Mankind, Forgive Our Foolish Ways

Men, find a church that sings.

Lead singing at home.

Take singing lessons if you need to.

Sing loud. Sing often. Sing with joy. Sing the truth. But one last thing needs to be said. Scripture makes it clear that men also need to learn to sing emotional songs, not just the ones that connect with their inner testosterone.

Let this be an encouragement to pastors to lead their men to sing—and to sing with all their masculine powers.

Sing, you men!

Questions

1. Why are many men turned off by modern worship songs?
2. Is this an excuse for men not to sing? If not, what's the remedy?

Recommended Hymn: "Rise Up, O Men of God"

CHAPTER 11

SING AS A CRITICAL DISCIPLESHIP TOOL

> *Let the word of Christ dwell in you richly in all wisdom, teaching and admonishing one another in psalms and hymns and spiritual songs, singing with grace in your hearts to the Lord. And whatever you do in word or deed, do all in the name of the Lord Jesus, giving thanks to God the Father through Him.*
> *—Col. 3:16-17*

Singing is a formational tool. When you sing, you are training followers of Jesus. When you sing, you are ministering to the whole flock. You are proclaiming the power of His name (Ps. 96:2).

Bob Kauflin put it this way: "Songs are de facto theology. They teach us who God is, what he's like, and how to relate to him."[1]

The hallmark New Testament charge to sing is found in Colossians 3:16-17. But this text does not stand in isolation; it

1. Bob Kauflin, *Worship Matters: Leading Others to Encounter the Greatness of God* (Wheaton, IL: Crossway Books, 2008), 92.

exists within the flow of the discipleship context of Colossians 3:1-17. The chapter begins with: "If then you were raised with Christ, seek those things which are above, where Christ is, sitting at the right hand of God" (Col. 3:1). Then the rest of the chapter defines what it looks like to "seek those things."

It involves setting your mind on things above (v. 2). It involves putting "to death your members which are on the earth: fornication, uncleanness, passion" (v. 5). Seeking the things above includes pursuing love: "put on tender mercies, kindness, humility, meekness, longsuffering; bearing with one another, and forgiving one another" (vv. 12-13).

Finally, Paul urges the church to "let the word of Christ dwell in you richly in all wisdom," which includes singing (vv. 16-17). In other words, singing is one of many components of church life designed to make disciples by being saturated in God's Word.[2]

The context of this is a corporate setting—"to the saints and faithful brethren in Christ who are in Colosse" (Col. 1:2). It is clear that Paul assumes there is a corporate gathering when he writes. His message is this: the Word of Christ "must dwell richly" as the congregation sings.

The song is the delivery system of the truth of the Word of God. Augustine explained the danger of singing while missing the truth being sung:

> *When it happens to me to be more moved by the singing than by what is sung, I confess myself to have*

---

2. Scott Aniol, "Singing That Sets Our Affections Above," *By the Waters of Babylon* (blog), May 29, 2024. https://g3min.org/singing-that-sets-our-affections-above/. Accessed August 1, 2025.

> *sinned criminally, and then I would rather not have heard the singing.*[3]

What is the Word of Christ? It is the entire testimony of the written Word of God. The Bible declares that God spoke in times past through the prophets, and thus every word of the Bible is a word of Jesus Christ, and we are to think His thoughts after Him (Heb. 1:1; 2 Cor. 10:5). The words of our songs should deliver reflections of the words of God.

The more richly the Word of Christ dwells in our hearts, the better the singing. Conversely, the more richly the Word is contained in the song, the more richly our hearts are fortified.

Our singing should be saturated with the Word of Christ. This means that the value of our singing is a direct result of either the richness or poverty of the Word of God in the song.

This only works when we sing songs rich in biblical truth. When we sing, we should be asking: "What is God trying to teach me about myself, the world, the church, and everything else?" And: "What is God trying to teach me to feel?" And: "What is God trying to motivate me to do?"

So, receive the Word, take it in, and let it take root. Hang on the words. Let them penetrate your innermost being. Chew the cud. Meditate on it. Fill your heart with the treasuries of Scripture.

Singing like this is a mark of discipleship. Paul tells us that these is the kind of disciples we are meant to be—singing disciples—making disciples as we sing, teaching and admonishing one another.

Sing as a critical discipleship tool.

---

3. Augustine, *Confessions*, XXXIII.50.

Questions

1. What does it mean to "richly dwell" in the songs we sing?
2. What are we doing for one another when we sing together as a congregation?

Recommended Hymn: "How Firm a Foundation"

CHAPTER 12

SING TO TEACH ONE ANOTHER

Let the word of Christ dwell in you richly in all wisdom, teaching and admonishing one another in psalms and hymns and spiritual songs, singing with grace in your hearts to the Lord. —Col. 3:16

The words in Colossians 3:16 explain that our singing has a goal: to teach and admonish one another. The Greek word for teaching is *didasko*, which means to provide instruction in a formal or informal setting.[1] We are to remind and admonish one another because our souls need correction and our thinking and feelings need to be modified. We are to "sing with understanding." This means we are to activate others through our singing.

This is just one reason that singing is such a treasure. Singing is theological training set to melody. Singing each note

1. Strong's G1321: διδάσκω (didaskō), to hold discourse with others in order to instruct them, deliver didactic discourses. Definition from Joseph Henry Thayer, *A Greek-English Lexicon of the New Testament* (New York: American Book Co., 1889).

and word is like the driving of a nail with a hammer, deep into the consciousness, like saturating the soul with truth.

The best songs are like a traffic jam of theology, Christology, soteriology, ecclesiology, eschatology, pneumatology, and cosmology. Songs are often countercultural and counter-emotional.

In Colossians 3:16, Paul is not telling the church to sing to "an audience of one" or to raise hands in our own private worlds before God alone. He is saying: "No, *you are also singing to the other people in the congregation*."

You are teaching your brothers and sisters.

You are planting seeds. You are watering gardens. You are changing hearts. You are shifting thinking. You are moving mountains. How? Because the melodies and lyrics are carrying doctrine, flowing like a spring.

When we sing the praises of God, we build up our neighbors in their walk through this world. And they need it just as much as we do. That's why Martin Luther said: "God doesn't need our good works, but our neighbor does."[2]

Your neighbor needs you to sing. He needs inspiration. He needs instruction. He needs you to belt it out.

Singing is a subcategory of biblical fellowship. The Greek word Paul uses for "fellowship" is the word *koinonia*, which refers to a complex interactive fellowship. It is horizontal and vertical simultaneously.[3] As we are in fellowship with the Lord, we are also in fellowship with one another (1 Cor. 1:9; Phil. 2:1; Acts 2:42; 2 Cor. 8:4). In this supernatural relationship, we are simultaneously connected on both

---

2. Gustaf Wingren, *Luther on Vocation* (Philadelphia: Muhlenberg Press, 1957), 10.

3. Strong's G2842: κοινωνία (koinōnía). Definition from *Thayer's Greek Lexicon*.

spiritual and relational planes with God and man. We are fellowshipping in our singing with one another. It is both horizontal—we look around; and vertical—we look up. And, in a sense, we carry each other with us.

This is in sharp contrast to some of the manifestations of contemporary Christian worship services in which a participant becomes lost in their personal emotions. Singing can become mindless, self-centered, narcissistic, and mesmerizing. When the mind is turned off toward your brothers and sisters, it does not reflect the fullness of Christian worship. It is simply ecstatic utterance.

In pagan worship, worshipers lose themselves in an altered state of emotional ecstasy. Mindless repetition fosters this. This is why George Harrison's song, "My Sweet Lord," repeats the words "Hare Krishna" over and over again. Hindu worship features mindless repetition for an ecstatic emotional state. The mind is turned off.

In Christian worship, we turn our minds on. We turn toward one another—we actually sing *to* one another and *with* one another.

Singing is a discipleship loop that includes inputting, savoring, and outputting:

1. Inputting: we receive the Word.
2. Savoring: we internalize the Word.
3. Outputting: we share the Word.

In Christian worship, each member has a responsibility to receive the truth of a song, sing it to God, sing it one another, sing it to one's own soul, and sing it to unbelievers. These things are done simultaneously.

Sing to teach one another.

Questions

1. Why is congregational singing *not* directed to an audience of one?
2. What is each member's responsibility when they sing in corporate worship?

Recommended Hymn: "Brethren, We Have Met to Worship"

CHAPTER 13

SING IN THE VOICE THE SONG IS WRITTEN IN

I will bless the Lord *at all times;*
His praise shall continually be in my mouth.
My soul shall make its boast in the Lord*;*
The humble shall hear of it and be glad.
Oh, magnify the Lord *with me,*
And let us exalt His name together. —Ps. 34:1-3

Notice the voice in which Psalm 34:1-3 is written and to whom it is sung. As we sing, we should observe whether the song we are singing is a testimony to the whole congregation or not.

- Is it sung personally *to God*?
- Is the song *about God*?
- Is the song declaring a doctrine?
- Is the song proclaiming a blessing?
- Is it a song that you sing to your own soul?

Songs in hymnbooks (and in the Bible) are written from various perspectives. Some are written in the first person: "Be Thou *MY* Vision."

Others are written in the second person in the form of questions: "Are *YOU* Washed in the Blood?"

Still others are corporate declarations: "O God, *OUR* Help in Ages Past."

Singing has such a diversity of factors to it. On the surface it seems simple, but the Bible reveals that God has designed a complex and beautiful tapestry of elements. Singing Christianly is to sing with depth of understanding and feeling. Christian singing is both self-conscious and intentional. It is complex, yet highly relational.

This is why we should be conscious of the voice in which a song is written.

- Is the psalm sung in the first person?
- Is it praise directed to God alone?
- It is an exhortation to the church?
- Is it an exhortation to your own soul?
- Is it a warning to the unbeliever?
- Is it a warning to the whole church?

Luther's stirring anthem, "A Mighty Fortress Is Our God," boldly proclaims:

A mighty Fortress is our God,
A Bulwark never failing;
Our Helper He amid the flood
Of mortal ills prevailing:
For still our ancient foe
Doth seek to work us woe;
His craft and power are great,

And, armed with cruel hate,
On earth is not his equal.

When we gather to sing, many of the songs are written to be sung to God alone. This is a tremendous help to us. In these songs we stand as individuals before God. We are "before the throne of God above." This is such a helpful awareness. There we are, with all our thoughts, with all our weaknesses and desires. It is as if no one else is there.

I stand amazed in the presence
Of Jesus the Nazarene,
And wonder how He could love me,
A sinner condemned unclean.

How marvelous! how wonderful!
And my song shall ever be . . .

The hymn "Great Is Thy Faithfulness" is another example of this:

Great is Thy faithfulness, O God my Father;
There is no shadow of turning with Thee;
Thou changest not, Thy compassions, they fail not;
As Thou hast been, Thou forever wilt be.

Great is Thy faithfulness!
Great is Thy faithfulness!
Morning by morning new mercies I see;
All I have needed Thy hand hath provided:
Great is Thy faithfulness, Lord, unto me!

The voice and style of a song should affect the *way* we sing the song as well. Some songs are somber and should be sung with seriousness and solemnity. Others are joyful and should be belted out with a big smile! Don't be a wooden singer who sings a song of joy as if it were a funeral dirge, but also don't be the kid who screams at the top of his lungs when gleefully singing of suffering either.

Here's an illustration: Some species of birds are able to sing two different tunes at the same time. This is true for the canary, the wood thrush, the nightingale, and the mockingbird. These songbirds from the passerine group (also called "perching birds") have a unique vocal organ called the syrinx. Unlike the human voice box (larynx), the syrinx has two independent halves, which allows birds to produce two different pitches at the same time. They literally sing a harmonic blend or duet with themselves. They are able to switch rapidly between notes with incredible control. They can sing two notes in harmony through one voice box.

In similar fashion, the disciple of Christ is called to live in dual harmony: singing to God while teaching one another (Col. 3:16).

In other words, when rightly pursued, singing is:

- Emotionally rich
- Intellectually deep
- Theologically sound
- Relationally connected
- Evangelistically self-conscious

As you sing, be self-conscious. Understand in what voice the song is written. To whom are you singing? If it's in the first person, search your own heart. If it's in the second person, be thoughtful of others included in the song. If it's in the third person, be relational. Always be aware of what you are singing about.

When we sing in the voice the song is written, we enter into the beautiful complexity of singing. We sing with one voice for double, triple, or quadruple purposes. To say it another way, singing is vertical (to God), horizontal (to one another) and internal (to yourself).

As we sing to God, to one another, to our own souls, and to the unbeliever among us, we are singing like songbirds.

Sing in the voice the song is written in.

Questions

1. How should the voice a song is written in affect the way we sing?
2. What does it mean for a believer to sing with "dual harmony" like songbirds?

Recommended Hymn: "O Worship the King"

CHAPTER 14

SING TO ADMONISH

Therefore do not be unwise, but understand what the will of the Lord is. And do not be drunk with wine, in which is dissipation; but be filled with the Spirit, speaking to one another in psalms and hymns and spiritual songs, singing and making melody in your heart to the Lord, giving thanks always for all things to God the Father in the name of our Lord Jesus Christ. —Eph. 5:17-20

You may be one of those people who doesn't like to tell people what to do. Some people are just like that! It's their personality. They hate confrontation. This is one reason why God commanded singing in His church. Singing is a corrective action. Many songs engage the believer in the act of admonishing. When we sing, we minister to one another by issuing commands. At least, that's what God had in mind. Each person is issuing commands to others.

The Greek word for admonishing is *noutheteo* or *nouthetic*, which literally means "to put in mind."[1] The term

1. Strong's G3560: νουθετέω (noutheteō). Definition from *Thayer's Greek Lexicon*.

"nouthetic counseling" was coined from this word. It means to warn, to advise someone of some danger, to inform of consequences, and to correct one another. *Nouthesia* is an action that seeks to move someone from one position to another, to warn and redirect. Our hearts need redirection.

Notice the admonitions in the following hymns:

- "Take Time to be Holy"
- "Sing the Wondrous Love of Jesus"
- "Stand Up, Stand Up for Jesus"
- "All Creatures of Our God and King"

Consider these lines from "All People That on Earth Do Dwell":

All people that on earth do dwell,
Sing to the Lord with cheerful voice;
Him serve with fear, His praise forthtell,
Come ye before him and rejoice.

"Take Time to Be Holy" is an admonition we sing to admonish one another:

Take time to be holy, speak oft with thy Lord;
Abide in Him always, and feed on His Word.
Make friends of God's children, help those
who are weak,
Forgetting in nothing His blessing to seek.

There are many songs that we sing for admonishment.

When a person sings "Bless the Lord, O My Soul," he is admonishing his own soul. Other songs also help to admonish us when we are falling short of what we are singing, such as "All I Have Is Christ," "As the Deer," and "My Jesus, I Love Thee."

Some people think it's hypocritical to sing things like "My Jesus, I Love Thee" when they are at a low point in their spiritual walk. This is a mistake. It's okay to sing something that you are struggling to attain. Let the song take you there. Through the song, the Lord wants to take you to a better place, so He has you sing the words. Perhaps your heart will catch up with them.

Let the song correct you, redirecting you and the whole church.

When we sing, we help one another to "Bless the Lord" and to "forget not all His benefits" (Ps. 103:1-2).

"Brethren, We Have Met to Worship"

Brethren, we have met to worship
And adore the Lord our God;
Will you pray with all your power,
While we try to preach the Word?
All is vain unless the Spirit
Of the Holy One comes down;
Brethren, pray, and holy manna
Will be showered all around. . . .

Let us love our God supremely,
Let us love each other, too;
Let us love and pray for sinners,
Till our God makes all things new.

Then He'll call us home to heaven,
At His table we'll sit down;
Christ will gird Himself and serve us
With sweet manna all around.

Sing to admonish.

Questions

1. Are you the kind of person who doesn't like to tell others what to do?
2. What does the word "admonish" mean?

Recommended Hymn: "Take Time to Be Holy"

CHAPTER 15

SING TO HELP YOU REMEMBER

When I remember You on my bed,
I meditate on You in the night watches.
Because You have been my help,
Therefore in the shadow of Your wings I will rejoice.
My soul follows close behind You;
Your right hand upholds me. —Ps. 63:6-8

Singing produces powerful mental interactions; it helps us remember words like no other activity does.[1] It embeds lyrics in the brain. This is both positive and negative. Singing impresses both truth and error, embedding it into the deepest corners of our thinking. This is why singing can help us learn the alphabet, the books of the Bible, the Ten Commandments, etc.

Singing simultaneously activates multiple parts of the brain. It enhances memory. It expands retention. It connects the brain in more ways than speaking and reading do.

1. Bob Kauflin, *Worship Matters: Leading Others to Encounter the Greatness of God* (Wheaton, IL: Crossway Books, 2008), 99.

Here is the scientific explanation: When you sing, your brain is active in several dimensions, including the auditory cortex (hearing and processing sound); the motor cortex (controlling the muscles used to produce the sound); emotional centers, like the amygdala; and memory-related areas like the hippocampus.[2] The interplay between so many various parts of the brain literally engraves the memory of the songs—and their messages—in our minds.

In other words, music is not confined to a single "music center" in the brain. Rather, it engages multiple cognitive systems—auditory, motor, memory, and emotional. This is why Victoria Williamson, a cognitive neuroscientist, says: "Music is a rich cognitive experience that engages many parts of the brain at once, including those for emotion, memory, movement, and attention."[3]

Music processing is distributed across both hemispheres of our brains. The brain treats music as a "whole-brain workout," observes Williamson. "Music is not a 'one-stop-shop' in the brain. . . . Instead, it is more like a city-wide festival, involving multiple areas across both hemispheres."[4]

The interplay between words and tunes forms a powerful shaping force in our consciousness. We all experience this: all of a sudden an unprofitable song starts up in your head that you haven't heard for many years. Where did it come from?

---

2. Artist Weekly Staff, "The Biology and Brainpower Behind Great Singing," *Artist Weekly*, April 15, 2025. https://artistweekly.com/the-biology-and-brainpower-behind-great-singing/. Accessed July 14, 2025. Sascha Frühholz, Wiebke Trost, Didier Grandjean, "The role of the medial temporal limbic system in processing emotions in voice and music," *Progress in Neurobiology*, Volume 123, December 2014, 1-17.

3. Victoria Williamson, *You Are the Music: How Music Reveals What It Means to Be Human* (London: Icon Books Ltd, 2014), 23.

4. Williamson, *You Are the Music*, 24.

It may happen in the middle of the night, and you can't get it out of your mind even though you are praying, "God change my mind; get my mind back on better thoughts!"

The Bible makes it clear that songs come back to you after many years. At the end of his life, Moses taught the children of Israel a song. God commanded him to teach this song on the final day of his life. He obeyed the Lord and did so. God had a distinctive purpose for teaching the Israelites that song. He knew that if they sang the words, they would never forget them. The Lord said:

> *Then it shall be, when many evils and troubles have come upon them, that this song will testify against them as a witness; for it will not be forgotten in the mouths of their descendants. (Deut. 31:21)*

This is one reason why music blended with singing is so powerful. If we sing good songs, good things will be stored in our hearts. If we sing bad songs, our hearts will be shaped by them. We ought to be very careful what we sing. Bob Kauflin offers this warning: "Sing words that God wants us to remember."[5]

This is so important because the songs that you sing will carry you through the ups and downs of life. And they will even affect your family members for many generations. Songs are powerful forces both for good and for ill. If your mind is filled with silly, ridiculous songs, such things will shape you. You will likely become a silly person. If your mind is full of immoral songs, you will want to be immoral. If your mind is filled with "psalms, hymns and spiritual songs," you will

---

5. Bob Kauflin, "Words of Wonder."

become, by God's grace, the holy person you desire to be. So don't forget to sing the things you really want to remember!

Sing to help you remember.

Questions

1. What parts of the brain does singing engage?
2. Since music is such a powerful memory aid, what kind of songs should we sing?

Recommended Hymn: "Be Thou My Vision"

CHAPTER 16

SING STRONG WITH GUSTO

Sing aloud to God our strength;
Make a joyful shout to the God of Jacob. —Ps. 81:1

In Psalm 98:4-6, we are commanded to actually shout when we sing. The divine singing teacher has spoken.

Shout joyfully to the Lord, *all the earth;*
Break forth in song, rejoice, and sing praises.
Sing to the Lord *with the harp,*
With the harp and the sound of a psalm,
With trumpets and the sound of a horn;
Shout joyfully before the Lord, *the King.*

Our singing carries our affection, not just notes (Isa. 5:1). Think of a bird in spring. Birds are not just making noise; they are calling out with purpose and energy. Think of an energetic pianist or violinist. They don't merely play the instrument; they pour themselves into the music.

In Nehemiah 12:42, the singers "sang loudly with Jezrahiah the director."

In Psalm 47:1, we are told to not only shout but to clap our hands: "Oh, clap your hands, all you peoples! Shout to God with the voice of triumph!"

The Outline of Biblical Usage explains what *shout* means: "raise a sound, cry out, give a blast; to shout a war-cry or alarm of battle; to sound a signal for war or march; to shout in triumph (over enemies)."[1]

This means we are not left to ourselves to figure out how to sing. God tells the church to sing "aloud." God tells us to sing strongly and with gusto—and happily.

In Psalm 100:1, the type of shout is specified: "Make a joyful shout to the Lord, all you lands! Serve the Lord with gladness. Come before His presence with singing."

This shout is a joyful shout!

In Psalm 33:3, the singing is skillful yet accompanied with a shout: "Sing to Him a new song; play skillfully with a shout of joy."

In these texts, joy and volume are mingled. When you sing, go loud! No mumbling. No breathy singing! Lift up your voices. Lift the roof off.

This happened in the days of Nehemiah. The people were so loud that you could hear the singing far away:

> *Also that day they offered great sacrifices, and rejoiced, for God had made them rejoice with great joy; the women and the children also rejoiced, so that the joy of Jerusalem was heard afar off.* (Neh. 12:43)

However, to sing "aloud" and to "shout" is not the same as yelling out words. To preserve the beauty of singing, we should avoid raising the voice to unnatural, strained tones. It's not bellowing it out (or bellerin' if you live in the South). We especially don't want our children to bellow and draw

1. Strong's H7321: רוּעַ (rûwaʻ), definition from Larry Pierce, *Outline of Biblical Usage*, created for the Online Bible (Ontario: Online Bible Foundation).

inappropriate attention to themselves. It's distracting. They need to be coached. We need to instruct them to refrain from straining their voices and yelling the words, while at the same time instructing them to sing with gusto.

When teaching children, it is important to focus on elements of healthy singing such as posture, relaxed and open throat and jaw, lifted soft palate, proper diaphragmatic breathing, and good vowel formation. As children work on these things, the volume will come with time!

John Wesley said:

> *Sing* lustily, *and with a good courage. Beware of singing as if you were half dead, or half asleep; but lift up your voice with strength. Be no more afraid of your voice now, nor more ashamed of its being heard, than when you sung the songs of Satan.*[2]

So we conclude that singing assists the church to fulfill her purpose to enjoy God by singing "aloud." The Westminster Shorter Catechism describes it this way: "What is the chief end of man? Man's chief end is to glorify God, and to enjoy him forever."[3] We are commanded to sing with a shout of joy:

> *But let all those rejoice who put their trust in You;*
> *Let them ever shout for joy, because You defend them;*
> *Let those also who love Your name*
> *Be joyful in You. (Ps. 5:11)*

Sing strong with gusto!

---

2. John Wesley, "Directions for Congregational Singing," *The Works of the Reverend John Wesley*, A.M., Vol. VII (New York: J. Emory and B. Wauch, 1831), 609.

3. Westminster Shorter Catechism Q. 1.

Questions

1. What does "shout" mean in Scripture?
2. According to Psalm 33:3 and 100:1, what should fuel our shouting?

Recommended Hymn: "Shout to Jehovah, All the Earth"

CHAPTER 17

SING ON THE WAY TO CHURCH

I was glad when they said to me, "Let us go into the house of the LORD." –Ps. 122:1

The Songs of Ascents (Ps. 120-134) picture father and mother on their journey to Jerusalem with the children skipping all around. (The word "ascents" also means "stairs," indicating an upward journey.)[1] The children are kicking rocks—"Stay out of that puddle, little Isaac." They are making their way to offer sacrifices to the Lord in the temple. They are going up to the "mountain of the LORD" (Isa. 2:2). It is a singing family getting ready for the worship of the Father of delights.

Picture your family singing on the way to church. It's Sunday morning. You are in your house, then your car, and now you are singing.[2] This is the biblical pattern we see in

1. Strong's H4609: מַעֲלָה (maʻălâh). Definition from *Brown-Driver-Briggs Lexicon*.

2. Keith & Kristyn Getty, *Sing!*, 65.

the Songs of Ascents, songs for making your way to worship God on Mt. Zion.

There are fifteen psalms of ascent—Psalm 120-134—which are like a small hymnbook. Think of a chorus book. They are short and easily sung by memory.

Phil Johnson explains the range of subjects in the Songs of Ascents:

> *persecution* (Psalm 120); *hope* (121); *fellowship* (122); *supplication* (123); *thanksgiving* (124); *confidence* (125); *patience* (126); *prosperity* (127); *peace* (128); *martyrdom* (129); *repentance* (130); *humility* (131); *expectation* (132); *unity* (133); and *praise* (134).

"These are virtues that in many ways echo or parallel the fruit of the Spirit in Galatians 5," Johnson adds.[3]

In the center of this collection of psalms is Psalm 127, which addresses family life. Seven psalms of ascent come before it and seven after. Perhaps this is telling us that the central psalm is about home life, for home life is established by God to be the fountain of blessing for all of life. Strong family life is foundational for spiritual life in the church, for healthful life in the city, for dutiful life in the shop, for diligent life in the field, and for righteous life in the courts of governmental administration.

These psalms imply family life. Calvin defines the scope of "house" as: "The whole domestic order and government of

3. Phil Johnson, "The Song of a Truly Blessed Man (Ps. 127)," sermon, Grace Community Church, Sun Valley, California, April 15, 2012. https://www.thegracelifepulpit.com/sermons.aspx?code=2012-04-15-PJ.

the family . . . not only a building of wood or stone but also the general state of the whole commonwealth."[4]

There is evidence that whole families from various Israelite communities would make their way together to Jerusalem to worship, singing these psalms. Likely there would be multiple families, along with many other travelers, making the pilgrimage.

All of the basic elements of home life are mentioned in Psalms 127 and 128. One element is seen as the most important of all: happy home life springs from the fear of the Lord and walking in His ways. Great dependence upon God is the secret of a blessed home life that reflects the love of Christ.

Matthew Henry has captured the essence of Psalm 128 by saying that it is:

> *. . . a psalm for families. In that we were taught that the prosperity of our families depends upon the blessing of God; in this we are taught that the only way to obtain that blessing which will make our families comfortable is to live in the fear of God and in obedience to him.*[5]

As you make your way to church for the worship of God on the Lord's Day, don't forget to sing with your family: "I was glad when they said to me, 'Let us go into the house of the LORD'" (Ps. 122:1). Create an atmosphere of praise for your family. Set wonderful expectations. Create excitement and expectation for what is to come.

Sing on your way to church.

---

4. John Calvin, *Commentary on the Book of Psalms*, vol. 5 (Bellingham, WA: Logos Bible Software, 2010), 105.

5. Henry, *Commentary on the Whole Bible*, on Psalm 128.

Questions

1. What fifteen psalms were sung as God's people made their way to worship?
2. How then should we lead our families as we're on the way to church?

Recommended Hymn: "Come, Christians, Join to Sing"

CHAPTER 18

SING TO PROCLAIM TRUTH

I will sing of mercy and justice; to You, O Lord, I will sing praises. —Ps. 101:1

Anchored! That's what singing can make you. In a world searching for what to believe and then making it up on their own or following another fallen human child of Adam, the Christian has a steady anchor—Truth. When we sing, we are making truth claims. We explain matters of biblical doctrine. We declare realities of history. All of this defines what we believe. Singing causes us to verbalize what we think and how we feel about God, the world, and ourselves. We are anchored by the Rock of Ages.

Just as we are called to pray with understanding, we should sing with understanding, too (1 Cor. 14:15). It's not enough to follow the melody. Our minds and hearts must also engage with the meaning of the words. Otherwise we're just performing music, not worshiping. Imagine someone operating a machine without knowing what it's for. In Christianity, there is no such thing as singing without truth.

In contrast, before we became Christians, we sang lots of songs that did not declare truth. When you are saved, the first thing you do when you come into the church is to sing. You sing the truth.

In Isaiah 35:6, the new believer is portrayed as singing: "And the tongue of the mute [shall] sing for joy" (ESV). Before salvation, they had "the tongue of the mute." But when they are converted, they then sing. They declare their identity like they never did before.

What are these new believers identifying with? Put simply, with truth. This is why singing is a defense of the truth.

Singing also reveals what is important to a church. When we sing in our corporate worship, we are declaring many important truths, including:

- What kind of God we worship: "Holy, Holy, Holy"
- What kind of gospel we are proclaiming: "Grace, Grace, God's Grace"
- What the basis of our unity is: "Blest Be the Tie that Binds"
- What kind of expectations we have: "O Come, O Come, Emmanuel"
- What kind of feelings we desire: "Jesus, the Joy of Loving Hearts"
- What kind of messages we want to proclaim to one another: "Praise Him, Praise Him"
- What kind of church we desire to be: "Brethren, We Have Met to Worship"
- What we want to say to one another: "A Mighty Fortress is Our God"

In addition, we are also declaring truth claims, defining what kind of people we want to be when we step outside of our church. We want to depart, girded with the belt of truth, happy in Him, consoled by Him, helped along in sorrow, and corrected by Him. We depart with songs ringing in our ears. We are anchored in truth.

It's very important for human beings to understand the truth claims of our identity. They affirm. They steady. They encourage. When we sing, we are verbalizing what we believe, what we know to be true. We are declaring who God is. We are verbalizing who we are and what kind of people we want to be. When we do this, we proclaim truth. We are not lost in space. We are tethered to everlasting truth.

Sing to proclaim truth.

Questions

1. How does singing steady your anchor?
2. How does proclaiming the truth through song help us in our walk?

Recommended Hymn: "A Mighty Fortress Is Our God"

CHAPTER 19

SING WITH THE LORD JESUS

"I will declare Your name to My brethren;
In the midst of the assembly I will sing praise to You."
—Heb. 2:12

On the evening when Christ was betrayed, He sang with His disciples (Matt. 26:30). Imagine what it was like to sing with the Lord Himself!

In Zephaniah 3 we are told that the Lord Himself, God the Father, sings over His church.

Sing, O daughter of Zion!
Shout, O Israel!
Be glad and rejoice with all your heart,
O daughter of Jerusalem! . . .
The LORD your God in your midst,
The Mighty One, will save;
He will rejoice over you with gladness,
He will quiet you with His love,
He will rejoice over with you with singing.
(Zeph. 3:14, 17)

Commenting on this remarkable passage, Keith Mathison states:

> *Stop and consider this for a moment. The Lord God Almighty, the Creator of heaven and earth, the Holy One of Israel, rejoices over the remnant. He exults over the faithful with loud singing. Loud singing! Rejoicing! This is not Aristotle's "Unmoved Mover." This is not the abstract god of the philosophers. This is our God, the God of Abraham, Isaac, and Jacob, the Father of our Lord Jesus Christ. And this God, the living God, rejoices over His faithful remnant with gladness and loud singing.*[1]

We see in the book of Revelation that our Lord Jesus is walking among the lampstands, dressed like the high priest of the Old Testament:

> *. . . in the midst of the seven lampstands One like the Son of Man, clothed with a garment down to the feet and girded about the chest with a golden band. . . . who walks in the midst of the seven golden lampstands. (Rev. 1:13; 2:1)*

Jesus is walking where His people are meeting—all over the world.

Matthew 18:20 also makes it clear that whenever the church meets, Christ is with us. And He never misses a meeting. He is like a bridegroom rejoicing over His bride (Isa. 62:5). He is present when we sing.

---

1. Keith Mathison, "Heaven Rejoices," Ligonier.org, December 31, 2009, https://learn.ligonier.org/articles/heaven-rejoices. Accessed August 1, 2025.

The writer of Hebrews tells us that Jesus Christ, the second person of the Trinity, is Himself singing with His people:

> *For both He who sanctifies and those who are being sanctified are all of one, for which reason He is not ashamed to call them brethren, saying:*
>
> *"I will declare Your name to My brethren;*
> *In the midst of the assembly I will sing praise to You."*
>
> *And again:*
>
> *"I will put My trust in Him."*
>
> *And again:*
>
> *"Here am I and the children whom God has given Me." (Heb. 2:10-13)*

It is clear that our Lord Jesus Christ is not ashamed to be among His people and to sing along with them. He still sings with us in spite of our weaknesses.

We may have lost our delight, but God the Father and the Lord Jesus Christ have not lost their delight in their people. The Lord Jesus is not only singing with us, but He is also singing through us:

> *Jesus sang while on earth. He still sings in heaven. He sings* through *us. When Christ dwells richly in us, we're filled with musical Wisdom to teach and admonish in song (Colossians 3:16). The Chief Singer sounds through each singer, making the choir's voice an enrichment of the Choirmaster's, the polyphony of the* totus Christus.[2]

---

2. Peter Leithart, "The God Who Sings," *Theopolis*, May 25, 2020, https://theopolisinstitute.com/leithart_post/the-god-who-sings/.

Robert Jenson remarks:

> *A congregation singing a hymn of praise to the Father is doubling the Son's praise, and the surge of rhythm and melody is the surge of the Spirit's glorification of the Father and the Son.*[3]

We often lose sight of the affection God has for us. But God does not! He is resting in His unchangeable love. We are not under condemnation for our faults. There is no one who can bring a charge against His elect. He sees us cleansed. He marks us as justified in Him.

He delights in the salvation of His people, and His mercies are cascading upon us as we sing: "For as the heavens are high above the earth, so great is His mercy toward those who fear Him" (Ps. 103:11).

He sings with delight—in us! Isaiah speaks of His delight and His joy in us, calling us "Hephzibah" (which means "my delight is in her"), declaring that "as a bridegroom rejoices over the bride, so shall your God rejoice in you" (Isa. 62:4-5).[4]

The song "How Firm a Foundation" is one such example of this:

> *Fear not, I am with thee, O be not dismayed,*
> *For I am thy God, and will still give thee aid;*
> *I'll strengthen thee, help thee, and cause thee to stand,*
> *Upheld by my righteous, omnipotent hand.*
>
> *When through the deep waters I call thee to go,*
> *The rivers of sorrow shall not overflow;*

---

3. Robert W. Jenson, *Systematic Theology, Volume 1: The Triune God* (Oxford University Press, 1997), 235.

4. Strong's H2567: חֶפְצִי בָהּ (Chephtsîy bâhh). Definition from *Brown-Driver-Briggs Lexicon*.

> *For I will be near thee, thy troubles to bless,*
> *And sanctify to thee thy deepest distress.*

Finally, when you return home after a church service, you can say:

> *We sang with the Lord today. Yes, you heard it; the Lord Jesus sang with us. Not only that, but the people were singing to me. They spoke words of life to me. They sang melodies to me, to God, and to the unbelievers. But what was most amazing is that the Lord Himself sang with us.*

Sing with the Lord Jesus.

Questions

1. Whenever the church meets, who is there?
2. How should Christ's presence with us in singing affect us?

Recommended Hymn: "I Heard the Voice of Jesus Say"

CHAPTER 20

SING WITH YOUR WHOLE HEART

Sing, O daughter of Zion!
Shout, O Israel!
Be glad and rejoice with all your heart,
O daughter of Jerusalem!
—Zeph. 3:14, emphasis added

Singing engages the whole being—body, soul, mind, emotions—and heart. This is why heartless singing is defective singing. In Zephaniah 3:14, the prophet is commanding the people of God to engage their hearts. Similarly, the Apostle Paul taught the churches to sing with their hearts, "singing with grace in your hearts to the Lord" (Col. 3:16; cf. Eph. 5:18-20).

In John 4, we encounter the language of worshiping "in spirit and in truth." I take this to be equivalent to "with all your heart." In this chapter, Jesus tells the woman at the well she did not understand what it meant to worship God. Her life did not bear witness to true worship. Jesus says, "But the hour is coming, and now is, when the true worshipers will worship the Father in spirit and truth" (John 4:23).

We learn here that not all worship is true worship. Not all singing is heart worship. Not all worship is "in truth." This is why we see different manifestations of what has been called worship today. Here are two:

First, there is emotionless ritualism. This is unfeeling, robotic, obligatory, joyless ritual.

Second, there is ritualistic emotionalism. This is all feeling, performing, personal expressionism untethered to the truth.

Jesus describes to the woman the type of worshipers God is seeking: "the true worshipers will worship the Father in spirit and truth; for the Father is seeking such to worship Him" (John 4:23). This teaches us that worship is a personal, self-conscious activity. It's not like breathing, which is automatic. Worship is a deliberate, intentional activity that one sets oneself to do. Time is allocated. Space is identified. Activity is defined. The heart is engaged.

Jesus explains the heart of true worship: "God is Spirit, and those who worship Him must worship in spirit and truth" (John 4:24). Similarly, Paul instructed the Corinthian church: "I will sing with the spirit, and I will also sing with understanding" (1 Cor. 14:15).

The one who is worshiped, God, is Spirit.

Jesus is explaining God to the woman. He is engaging her in the theology of the worship of God.

The *content* of worship is "in truth." Worship is based on divine revelation—the truth. In this sense, it is true knowledge of the One True God.

In other words, true worship is focused on the true God. It is focused on what God is really like, not what we would like Him to be. Not what we feel. True worship has its object in the glory of God the Father, our Lord Jesus Christ, and the Holy Spirit.

Jesus is calling this woman's attention to the substance, not the form. To worship is to relish and delight in the truth about Him. To worship is to "taste and see that the LORD is good" (Ps. 34:8). This is the substance of worship.

The summary of the two elements of true worship is this: Spirit and truth, heart and head, doxology and theology. True worship includes sincerity of heart and orthodoxy. In Christianity, melodies are mixed with words. The two exist in harmony with one another.

God is seeking worshipers like this.

Matthew Henry, in his commentary on Colossians 3:16, remarks:

> *But, when we sing psalms, we make no melody unless we sing with grace in our hearts, unless we are suitably affected with what we sing and go along in it with true devotion and understanding. Singing of psalms is a teaching ordinance as well as a praising ordinance; and we are not only to quicken and encourage ourselves, but to teach and admonish one another, mutually excite our affections, and convey instructions.*[1]

God's design for singing is that we engage our whole heart. We are often in such a spiritual state that we sing dispassionately. We don't feel like singing. This is not a surprise to God for, "He knows our frame" (Ps. 103:14). He has made singing to reengage our heart even when we might not want to sing

1. Henry, *Commentary on the Whole Bible*, on Colossians 3:16.

or feel like singing. Singing, therefore, is a wonderful gift to exercise our hearts and activate our emotions.

Dietrich Bonhoeffer wrote: "The heart sings because it is overflowing with Christ."[2]

In John Wesley's "Directions for Singing," he gives very specific instructions:

> *Above all, sing* spiritually. *Have an eye to God in every word you sing. Aim at pleasing Him more than yourself, or any other creature. In order to do this, attend strictly to the sense of what you sing; and see that your heart is not carried away with the sound, but offered to God continually; so shall your singing be such as the Lord will approve here, and reward you when He cometh in the clouds of heaven.*[3]

As we have seen, Christian worship is both thoughtful and emotional. It acknowledges that we were created as complex human beings. Pagan worship makes an idol of emotions. On the other hand, lifeless, conservative Reformed worship may make an idol of doctrine to the absence of emotions.

But God calls for the whole person to participate. Both conservative and pagan worship can be lifeless.

Don't confuse emotional singing with lifegiving singing.

And don't confuse doctrinal singing with lifegiving singing.

God has designed us for both emotions and doctrine. This is why He commands both.

---

2. Dietrich Bonhoeffer, *Life Together* (London: SCM Press Ltd., 1954), 42.
3. John Wesley, *The Works of the Reverend John Wesley, A.M.*, Volume 14 (London: Wesleyan Conference Office, 1872), 346.

It is critical that the church be a teaching church. But our teaching does not only come through our preaching; it also comes through our singing.

One characteristic of human beings is that we sing what we love, and thus when you find a church which loves the teaching and preaching from the pulpit, you almost always find a church which loves to sing about the teaching. They sing because they love the doctrine which saturates their whole being.

The church is a place where the people believe that the Word of God is worth singing about.

Sing thoughtfully and emotionally—with your whole heart.

Sing with your whole heart.

Questions

1. According to John 4:24, what two elements accompany true singing?
2. What two ditches are we to avoid as we sing?

Recommended Hymn: "Breathe on Me"

CHAPTER 21

SING TO BE CHANGED

Create in me a clean heart, O God,
And renew a steadfast spirit within me. —Ps. 51:10

Singing Psalm 51 was designed to change your life. Do you want your life to be transformed? Then let God's treasury of songs change you. Let these songs correct you. Let them call you higher. Let the songs penetrate your sorrows. Let them heal your wounds. Let them be the balm of Gilead. Let them be goads to spur you onward. Let them break the chains and set you free. Sometimes we need the consolation of gentleness to move us. Sometimes we need shock treatment. The Psalms and the other songs in Scripture give us both.

Psalms, hymns, and spiritual songs are not safe. They don't leave you alone. They crash into your inner world, shaping loyalties, altering affections, changing worldviews, transforming minds, and shifting emotions. John Calvin called the book of Psalms "an anatomy of all the parts of the soul."[1]

We sing to express what we believe so that we might become what we sing.

---

1. John Calvin, *Commentary on the Book of Psalms*, trans. James Anderson (Calvin Translation Society, 1845), "Author's Preface," 1:xxxvii.

As we said earlier, songs are meant to teach us, admonish us, correct us, comfort us, mobilize us, and sustain us. Through the ups and downs of our lives, through every season of our lives, through the happy and the sad times, He has given us songs to change us.

Thoughtful, prayerful singing is the best corrective to pride, failure, fear, anxiety, anger, hurt feelings, and many other sins. How about the sin of distrust in God? Here is a psalm to snap us out of it: "Oh, taste and see that the LORD is good; blessed is the man who trusts in Him!" (Ps. 34:8).

Singing stirs up holy affections and awakens godly desires. Singing is helpful to change our emotions. In his book, *Religious Affections*, Jonathan Edwards explains:

> *And the duty of singing praises to God, seems to be appointed wholly to excite and express religious affections. No other reason can be assigned, why we should express ourselves to God in verse, rather than in prose, and do it with music, but only, that such is our nature and frame, that these things have a tendency to move our affections.*[2]

Everyone knows that music sharpens the affections and moves the emotions. It stirs the soul. But music accompanied with singing doubles the impact. It is emotionally charged speech.

How often has a song strengthened you, moved you, and changed your heart?

This is how singing is a means of sanctification. There are times when we just need to sing because singing songs from

---

2. Jonathan Edwards, *Religious Affections*, ed. Paul Ramsey (*WJE Online* Vol. 2 [1754]), 115. http://edwards.yale.edu/.

Scripture changes our hearts for the better. In singing we confess our sins, declare the power of God, express our trust, and recount His mercies.

There are several psalms in which the singer expresses his fear or despair. But by the time the song is over, fear and despair have given way to praise and thanksgiving (Ps. 3; 22; 31:9-24; 38; 73).

David acknowledged this through Psalm 147:1-3:

Praise the LORD!
For it is good to sing praises to our God;
For it is pleasant, and praise is beautiful.
The LORD builds up Jerusalem;
He gathers together the outcasts of Israel.
He heals the brokenhearted
And binds up their wounds.

Singing is the best antidote to pride, failure, fear, anxiety, anger, hurt feelings, and many other sins. It is a wonderful way to say, "Lord, change me."

Sing to be changed.

Questions

1. How is singing the best antidote to pride, failure, fear, anxiety, anger, and hurt feelings?
2. What are the ups and downs of your life right now, and how can singing address them?

Recommended Hymn: "Spirit of the Living God"

CHAPTER 22

SING TO YOUR OWN SOUL

Bless the LORD, O my soul;
And all that is within me, bless His holy name!
Bless the LORD, O my soul,
And forget not all His benefits:
Who forgives all your iniquities,
Who heals all your diseases,
Who redeems your life from destruction,
Who crowns you with lovingkindness and
tender mercies,
Who satisfies your mouth with good things,
So that your youth is renewed like the eagle's.
—Ps. 103:1-5

In the psalm above, David is singing to his own soul. He is asking the Lord to bless his soul—his innermost being—his unseen self! He uses beautiful poetic language, full of verbs, to acknowledge the neediness of his own soul—his spiritual need.

He desired his whole soul, his whole being, to bless the Lord.

Isaac Watts adapted Psalm 103:1-5 into a hymn:

O bless the Lord, my soul!
Let all within me join
And aid my tongue to bless his name
Whose favors are divine.

O bless the Lord, my soul,
Nor let his mercies lie
Forgotten in unthankfulness
And without praises die.

In another place, David's soul was cast down, so he sings to his soul:

Why are you cast down, O my soul?
And why are you disquieted within me?
Hope in God, for I shall yet praise Him
For the help of His countenance. (Ps. 42:5)

He was literally singing to himself!

In Psalm 146, David is calling his own soul to praise God:

Praise the Lord!
Praise the Lord, O my soul! (v. 1)

Then he declares his intention to praise the Lord:

While I live I will praise the Lord;
I will sing praises to my God while I have my being (v. 2)

In Lamentations 3:24-25, the tables are turned. The soul is talking to the believer:

"The Lord is my portion," says my soul,
"Therefore I hope in Him!"
The Lord is good to those who wait for Him,
To the soul who seeks Him.

Singing Christianly is to sing with depth to your own soul. It accomplishes several things at once. We are fellowshipping with God, our brethren, and our souls—all at the same time.

In this sense, Christian singing is meant to be self-consciously rich and diverse, even to the level of your soul. But Christian singing is far superior to secular. Lots of secular music includes singing to the soul but it often encourages sin, lust, depression, and anger. In contrast, Christian singing calls up the mortification of sin, Christian duty, holy love and sanctified emotions.

Sing to your own soul.

Questions

1. What did David sing to his own soul, and what did he emphasize?
2. How should this knowledge impact our approach to times of singing?

Recommended Hymn: "O Bless the Lord, My Soul"

CHAPTER 23

SING TO DO BATTLE

But I will sing of Your power;
Yes, I will sing aloud of Your mercy in the morning;
For You have been my defense
And refuge in the day of my trouble. —Ps. 59:16

Songs of war have nearly vanished from the church. Yet singing is war. The German Jesuit Adam Contzen (1620) remarked that Luther had converted more souls with his hymns than with all his books and sermons.[1]

Peter Leithart wrote:

> *When we sing Scripture's songs in the energy of the Spirit, we witness to heaven's soundscape and make principalities and powers tremble. The world, the flesh, and the devil strive to silence or distort this alien song. Satan wants the world to believe the devil has all the best music. Don't let him get away with it.*

1. "Hymni Lutheri animos plures, quam scripta et declamationes occiderunt." Adam Contzen, S.J., *Politicorum libri decem* (Mainz: Johannes Kinck, [1621?]), 2:100.

There is a modern song that captures this: "O church arise, and put your armor on."[2]

Why does the church lack songs of war in the 21st century? This makes no sense because when we sing, we enter into battle; we engage in spiritual warfare. Singing ushers every true believer to the front of the Devil's war against the soul. Singing is a defense of the truth. It casts down arguments raised up against Christ. It preserves the unity of the church.

The Bible is filled with songs for battle. Here are a few:

A Song for War

In 2 Chronicles 20:18-21, we have a song that arose out of preparation for war. This was the response of the Jews as the Moabites and Ammonites gathered to attack Judah. This song demonstrates that true worship in singing is spiritual warfare:

> *And Jehoshaphat feared, and set himself to seek the Lord, and proclaimed a fast throughout all Judah. So Judah gathered together to ask help from the Lord; and from all the cities of Judah they came to seek the Lord. . . . Now when they began to sing and to praise, the Lord set ambushes against the people of Ammon, Moab, and Mount Seir, who had come against Judah; and they were defeated.* (2 Chron. 20:3-4, 22)

2. Keith Getty and Stuart Townend, "O Church Arise," in *Sing! The Getty Music Worship Songbook* (Nashville: B&H Publishing, 2017).

Songs of Deliverance

The first song we encounter in the Bible is a song of rescue in time of war. "The Lord is my strength and my song; and He has become my salvation" (Exod. 15:2).

The Exodus is the most prominent, oft-repeated moment in the Bible. It is a picture of redemption from sin and the abusive authority of Pharoah.[3] Not only that, but Exodus 15 prefigures Revelation 15. This song of deliverance from bondage will also be sung at the end of the age, as we see in Revelation 15. David says, "You shall preserve me from trouble; You shall surround me with songs of deliverance" (Ps. 32:7).

In 2 Samuel 22 and Psalm 18, we see David singing a song of deliverance after God rescued him from the hand of his enemies.

In 1 Samuel 18:6-7, we observe the women singing after David's victory over Goliath:

> *Now it had happened as they were coming home, when David was returning from the slaughter of the Philistine, that the women had come out of all the cities of Israel, singing and dancing, to meet King Saul, with tambourines, with joy, and with musical instruments. So the women sang as they danced.*

---

3. D.A. Carson observed, "The Exodus is the greatest redemptive event in the Old Testament to which subsequent revelation points to again and again and again." D.A. Carson, "Exodus: Understanding One of the Bible's Major Themes," DesiringGod.org, August 4, 2016. https://www.desiringgod.org/interviews/exodus-understanding-one-of-the-bibles-major-themes. Accessed July 21, 2025.

A Song before Attack

In Isaiah 26, we witness a song of the Messiah and the captives He has set free. This entire chapter is a song that is meant to be sung before troubled times. It communicates to us that God is the God of all comfort who walks with His people in times of trouble. He gives them a song to sing: "In that day this song will be sung in the land of Judah, 'We have a strong city'" (Isa. 26:1).

There are various circumstances in which God allows His people to go through times of trouble. Often these times of trouble come because God is bringing judgment upon a nation or because the people of God are being oppressed. At other times, however, these times of trouble come when we have been foolish or sinful and are under the chastisement of the Lord. It is in this context that the song in Isaiah 26 appears.

This song answers an important question: "How should I prepare myself for a time of judgment? And when it comes, how will I be prepared for any reversal or calamity?"

In verse 1, we see that the song is to be sung at a particular time, "In that day." This day could be the day of the time of judgment, but it could also be the time of the gospel.

Calvin believed the Jews would sing this song to prepare themselves for the coming judgment and would use it to teach their children about it.

> *The Prophet composed for them this song, even before the calamity occurred, that they might be better prepared for enduring it, and might hope for better things. I do not think that it was composed solely that, when they had been delivered, they might give thanks to God, but that even during their captivity, though they were like dead men*

> *(Ezek. 37:1), they might strengthen their hearts with this confidence, and might also train up their children in this expectation, and hand down these promises, as it were to posterity.*[4]

Isaiah taught the people this song to help them keep their minds stayed on the kingdom of God. Even while they watched the collapse of their city, the walls broken down and the bulwarks in ruins, they would sing this song to help them see the plan of God and remember the glories to come.

A Song of Victory

In Judges 5, we find Deborah and the commander of the Israelite army singing a song of victory when they were delivered from the Canaanites after enduring twenty years of oppression.

> *Awake, awake, Deborah!*
> *Awake, awake, sing a song!*
> *Arise, Barak, and lead your captives away.* (Judg. 5:12)

Singing is a form of spiritual warfare.

When you come into the congregation to "present your bodies a living sacrifice, holy and acceptable to God," sing to do battle. Engage the battle over temptations, wrong emotions, and unbiblical beliefs. Sing against the powers and principalities. Sing for the delivery of sinners from the bondage of the Devil.

Sing to do battle!

---

4. John Calvin, *Commentary on the Book of the Prophet Isaiah*, vol. 2 (Bellingham, WA: Logos Bible Software, 2010), 208-209.

Questions

1. What songs of battle are found in Scripture, and what can we learn from them?
2. How does singing songs of battle in times of peace help us?

Recommended Hymn: "Onward, Christian Soldiers"

CHAPTER 24

SING IN EVERY SEASON OF LIFE

I will sing to the LORD as long as I live;
I will sing praise to my God while I have my being.
May my mediation be sweet to Him;
I will be glad in the LORD. —Ps. 104:33-34

In this psalm, we learn that we should be singing to the Lord our whole life long.

The reason we should sing through every season in life is simple: the Bible gives you a song for every season.[1]

God will see you through every predicament, every feeling, every hardship, every loss, every joy, every attack, every betrayal. The Bible is full of different kinds of songs. We should sing them all. The Lord meets us everywhere at every phase of our lives. Be the thankful person who looks back on your life and says, "Your statutes have been my songs in the house of my pilgrimage" (Ps. 119:54).

Here are some examples.

1. Keith and Kristyn Getty, *Sing!*, 41.

The Song of the Well: For Times of Privation

This is the song the Israelites sang in Numbers 21:16-18 when God provided water for them just before they were attacked by Sihon, king of the Amorites. They sang to the well: "Spring up, O well!" This is a song of provision in times when provision is scarce, and we are frightened.

The Song of Moses: For Times of Transition

God commanded Moses to write a song on the last day of his life as he was passing the mantle of leadership to Joshua. It is called the "Song of Moses" (Deut. 32), who "spoke in the hearing of all the assembly of Israel the words of this song until they were ended" (Deut. 31:30). It is a song of righteousness and mercy, judgment and grace, faithfulness and sovereignty.

A Song for the Sabbath Day: For the Day of Rest

In Psalm 92, we see a song that was sung for the Sabbath day:

> *It is good to give thanks to the LORD,*
> *And to sing praises to Your name, O Most High;*
> *To declare Your lovingkindness in the morning,*
> *And Your faithfulness every night, . . .*
> *To declare that the LORD is upright;*
> *He is my rock, and there is no unrighteousness in Him*
> *(Ps. 92:1-2, 15)*

A Song of Consecration: For Times of Dedication

We also find that singing occurred after a time of disobedience when the Ark of the Covenant was brought to Jerusalem in 1 Chronicles 15.

After incurring God's wrath for his initial disobedience, David was careful to regulate God's worship according to His commands, stating:

> *". . . sanctify yourselves, you and your brethren, that you may bring up the ark of the* Lord *God of Israel to the place I have prepared for it. For because you did not do it the first time, the* Lord *our God broke out against us, because we did not consult Him about the proper order." So the priests and the Levites sanctified themselves to bring up the ark of the* Lord *God of Israel. (1 Chron. 15:12-14)*

As they endeavored to follow the Lord in their worship of Him, David and the leaders of the Levites appointed singers and musicians so their singing would be full of joy:

> *Then David spoke to the leaders of the Levites to appoint their brethren to be the singers accompanied by instruments of music, stringed instruments, harps, and cymbals, by raising the voice with resounding joy. (1 Chron. 15:16)*

A Song of Rejoicing: For Times of Thanksgiving

In 2 Chronicles 29:28 we observe singing that was accompanied by trumpet playing: "So all the assembly worshiped, the singers sang, and the trumpeters sounded; all this continued until the burnt offering was finished."

A Song of Joy: For Times of Jubilation

In Psalm 100 we see the singing of the saints as they gather together before the Lord.

> *Make a joyful shout to the LORD, all you lands!*
> *Serve the LORD with gladness;*
> *Come before His presence with singing.*
> *Know that the LORD, He is God;*
> *It is He who has made us, and not we ourselves;*
> *We are His people and the sheep of His pasture.*
>
> *Enter into His gates with thanksgiving,*
> *And into His courts with praise.*
> *Be thankful to Him, and bless His name.*
> *For the LORD is good;*
> *His mercy is everlasting,*
> *And His truth endures to all generations. (Ps. 100:1-5)*

A Song of Gladness: For Times Celebrating God's Kindness

In Psalm 104:33-34, we see that we should be singing to the Lord our whole life long. As David states:

> *I will sing to the Lord as long as I live;*
> *I will sing praise to my God while I have my being.*
> *May my meditation be sweet to Him;*
> *I will be glad in the LORD.*

Servant Songs: For Times to Remember Jesus Christ

There are a total of four servant songs in Isaiah, all of which are prophesies of the coming Messiah. We sing about His coming, for it is worthy of our praise.

In beautiful poetic metaphor, Isaiah declares that even nature sang to the Messiah and, by implication, it sings to us, declaring His mercy when we are sent by the Lord:

For you shall go out with joy,
And be led out with peace;
The mountains and the hills
Shall break forth into singing before you,
And all the trees of the field shall clap their hands. (Isa. 55:12)

Sing, O heavens!
Be joyful, O earth!
And break out in singing, O mountains!
For the LORD has comforted His people,
And will have mercy on His afflicted. (Isa. 49:13)

A Song of Praise: For Times of Good News

King Hezekiah sings after receiving the good news that God has granted him fifteen more years of life following his sickness:

The LORD was ready to save me;
Therefore we will sing my songs with
stringed instruments
All the days of our life, in the house of the LORD. (Isa. 38:20)

Notice that these are songs Hezekiah seems to have written himself. He calls them "my songs," and he commits the nation to keep singing these songs in the house of the Lord till the end of his life.

Songs of Celebration: For Acknowledging God's Acts of Providence

In Ezra 3:10-13, we discover a song celebrating the restoration of what was lost. This occurred when Ezra and the Jews sang over the foundation of the temple which they had laid in Jerusalem after returning from seventy years of captivity. This song of restoration was also sung by Nehemiah and the Jews as they celebrated the completion of the wall around Jerusalem in Nehemiah 12:27-47. Their singing was so loud that "the joy of Jerusalem was heard afar off" (Neh. 12:43).

These large thanksgiving choirs led by Nehemiah and Ezra demonstrate that there are times when the people of God simply need to stop and give thanks—regardless of their current difficulties.

In Nehemiah 12 we see that, a month after the city wall around Jerusalem had been finished, the Jews were looking back in joyful celebration of what God had done over the last one hundred years. Having identified with the reformation which God had wrought among them, all the people—women and children included—rose up to dedicate themselves and the wall in joyful obedience.

> *Also that day they offered great sacrifices, and rejoiced, for God had made them rejoice with great joy; the women and the children also rejoiced, so that the joy of Jerusalem was heard afar off. (Neh. 12:43)*

Sing through all the seasons of your life.

Questions

1. Why do we sing in every season of life?
2. What are some seasons of life captured in song throughout Scripture?

Recommended Hymn: "Great Is Thy Faithfulness"

CHAPTER 25

SING THROUGH SUFFERING

Have mercy on me, O Lord, for I am weak;
O Lord, heal me, for my bones are troubled.
My soul also is greatly troubled;
But You, O Lord—how long? —Ps. 6:2-3

The Psalms make it clear that David suffered much. The Bible assumes that God's people will suffer. That is why there are approximately sixty psalms of lament or suffering. Yet He has kindly given us a way through the tears, the attacks, the betrayals, the reversals, the losses.

He provides songs that carry us through our sorrows. Dan Kreider notes, "The praise of Jesus Christ is a precious consolation in sadness, our weapon against the powers of darkness."[1]

When you read stories of the martyrs throughout history, many of them were singing through the flames. After Hus was condemned to death, he declared to his persecutors that they might "silence [this] goose, but a hundred years hence there will arise a swan whose singing you will not be able to

1. Dan Kreider, January 6 entry in: *Awake My Soul* (Jupiter, FL: Hymnworks, 2024).

silence."[2] Remarkably, 102 years later, Martin Luther nailed the Ninety-Five Theses to the door of Wittenburg Chapel.

Church tradition tells us that when Perpetua and Felicity walked into the Coliseum to face the wild animals and gladiators in the third century, they began singing a hymn. Then Perpetua straightened her hair with a hairpin in order not to look disheveled during her death. She was suffering, but she was strong in her suffering.[3]

A Song from the Pit

In Psalm 40, we are taught through David's cry how to sing when we find ourselves in a horrible pit:

> *I waited patiently for the LORD;*
> *And He inclined to me,*
> *And heard my cry.*
> *He also brought me up out of a horrible pit,*
> *Out of the miry clay,*
> *And set my feet upon a rock,*
> *And established my steps.*
> *He has put a new song in my mouth—*
> *Praise to our God;*
> *Many will see it and fear,*
> *And will trust in the LORD. (Ps. 40:1-3)*

---

2. J.A. Wylie, *History of Protestantism*, Vol. 1 (New York: Cassell and Company, 1879), 164.
3. W.H. Shewring, trans., *The Passion of Perpetua and Felicity, MM: A New Edition and Translation of the Latin Text* (London: Sheed and Ward, 1931), 37-42.

As John Newton asked: "Why should I fear in the darkest hour?"[4]

A Song of Prisoners

In Acts 16:25, we encounter a song sung by prisoners. After being arrested, Paul and Silas sang while confined in the Philippian jail. "But at midnight Paul and Silas were praying and singing hymns to God, and the prisoners were listening to them."

In James 5:13, we find that singing is an expression of cheerfulness. James states: "Is anyone among you suffering? Let him pray. Is anyone cheerful? Let him sing psalms."

In Matthew 26, we learn that we can have a song to sing even in our darkest hour just as Jesus sang a hymn with His disciples after sharing the Lord's Supper with them. After singing together as brothers, they went out to the Mount of Olives, where the peak of Jesus' suffering was about to begin. It would culminate when He was hung on the cross and cried: "My God, my God, why have You forsaken Me?" (Ps. 22:1-3).

> *"But I say to you, I will not drink of this fruit of the vine from now on until that day when I drink it new with you in My Father's kingdom." And when they had sung a hymn, they went out to the Mount of Olives. Then Jesus said to them, "All of you will be made to stumble because of Me this night, for it is*

4. This is the opening line to John Newton's hymn, "Jesus All and in All." Printed in the *Gospel Magazine*, June 1771, in 8 stanzas of 3 lines, headed "In uno Jesu omnia" and signed "Omicron." It was included in the *Olney Hymns*, 1779, Bk. iii., No. 46, with the heading "Jesus my All." Since that time it has been included in a large number of hymnbooks both old and new.

written: 'I will strike the Shepherd, and the sheep of the flock will be scattered.'" (Matt. 26:29-31)

A Song of Women in Distress

We should also notice the women who sang in the Bible. They experienced great difficulties and broke through to great victories.

The Song of Miriam arose out of a serious threat from the Egyptian army (Exod. 15:20-21).

The Song of Deborah arose out of fierce attacks from enemy nations (Judg. 5).

The Song of Hannah arose out of barrenness (1 Sam. 2:1-10).

The Song of Mary arose in the midst of ostracism for her pregnancy (Luke 1:46-55).

God even commands the barren woman to sing:

"Sing, O barren,
You who have not borne!
Break forth into singing, and cry aloud,
You who have not labored with child!
For more are the children of the desolate
Than the children of the married woman," says the LORD.
(Isa. 54:1)

We too can sing when we are in our darkest hour.

Some people try to avoid singing and preaching when they are in the midst of their greatest struggles, but that's a huge mistake! We too must sing during the hardest times of our lives. Our songs will carry us through as they teach, correct, comfort, mobilize, and sustain us through the ups and downs of our earthly walk. God gives His church songs to help His people through all those difficult times. Indeed, time would fail me to tell you of all the songs that have carried me through my personal times of trial.

When we come into the congregation to present our bodies a living sacrifice, holy and acceptable to God, *we come to sing—no matter what waves of sorrow are washing over us.*

> *My brethren, count it all joy when you fall into various trials, knowing that the testing of your faith produces patience. (James 1:2-3)*

Sing through suffering!

Questions

1. How many psalms did David write while suffering, and what should we learn from them?
2. Who are some of the people in the New Testament who sang during times of trial or sorrow?

Recommended Hymn: "It Is Well with My Soul"

CHAPTER 26

SING TO IMPACT PEOPLE AROUND YOU

Praise is awaiting You, O God, in Zion;
And to You the vow shall be performed.
O You who hear prayer,
To You all flesh will come. —Ps. 65:1-2

Singing is infectious. We sing, and everyone who hears us catches the infection.

Over and over, I've caught myself humming or singing a song, only to discover that someone in my house was whistling, humming, or singing it already.

I have a daughter who was a legend on this in our home. I would get in the car and catch myself singing a song—only to realize it was my daughter who was whistling or humming it in the house before I left. I got infected by her song.

Those songs were a blessing because they were always spiritual songs. I was glad she did not hum worldly songs. I don't want that! They carry me in the wrong direction.

I've also had the opposite experience of hearing someone singing an ungodly or ridiculous song, and I caught it—and then found myself thinking: "Lord, please stop my mind from singing this stupid song!"

In a home we should be careful what we sing, hum, and whistle. We may be the reason a child, sibling, or parent has been influenced by silliness—or worse.

The spiritual songs we sing continue with us, for:

- What we sing at church is what we hum in our hearts
- What we hum in our hearts is what we sing in our homes
- What we sing in our homes, we will belt out in our cars
- What we belt out in our cars, we hum while we work
- What we hum while at work, we will hum when we get home
- What we hum at home, others will start to sing as well

Singing is infectious, and others can catch the infection—at home, at church, at work—everywhere.

Sing to impact the people around you.

Questions

1. Have you ever heard someone hum or sing a song, and then you started singing it? Give an example.
2. Since singing impacts others, what kind of songs should you sing?

Recommended Hymn: "Blessed Assurance"

CHAPTER 27

SING THE PSALMS

God gave the church a hymnal with 150 songs. It is the best hymnal ever printed. These songs are inerrant and authoritative. There are many theological, historical, and practical reasons the church should sing out of the Psalms.

Psalm-singing is experiencing a resurgence in the 21st century. This is a good trend, for the Psalms are designed by God to be the hymnal of the people of God. I am not an "exclusive psalmodist." I believe Scripture implies that God energizes His people throughout the centuries to write songs. And it seems to me that the mention of "psalms, hymns, and spiritual songs" (Eph. 5:19) refers to the many kinds of songs in the Bible. There are many songs in the Bible that are not in the Psalter. For example, we have the songs of Isaiah, Moses, and John (as recorded in Revelation).

However, it is a mistake to ignore the Psalter.

First, this is the hymnbook of the church.

Second, the New Testament commands the church to sing psalms (Eph. 5:19; Col. 3:16).

Third, these are divinely inspired songs (2 Tim. 3:16).

Fourth, next to Isaiah, Psalms is the most highly quoted book in the New Testament.[1]

Fifth, many of the psalms are Christological, pointing to Christ.[2] Jesus said: "These are the words which I spoke to you while I was still with you, that all things must be fulfilled which were written in the Law of Moses and the Prophets and the Psalms concerning Me" (Luke 24:44).

Sixth, the Psalms cover the whole range of human experiences.[3]

Seventh, the Psalms are emotionally formational.

Eighth, the Psalms offer a countercultural depth and emotional expression that is lacking in many modern worship songs. There is a psalm for every feeling you will ever have, every difficulty you will ever face, every enemy you will ever encounter. It is a compendium for every situation.

Bob Kauflin sums up the different kinds of psalms as follows:

> *They can be short, long, or somewhere in between (Psalms 117; 119; 89). They can enable us to speak to God, others, or ourselves, sometimes in the same psalm (Psalms 86; 100; 62:5-7; 42). We have psalms about God and about us (Psalms 145; 133). And when it comes to first-person pronouns, Psalm 71 contains*

1. Isaiah is quoted or alluded to 412 times, with the Psalms at 404. Rick Brannan and Jeffrey Glen Jackson, *New Testament Use of the Old Testament* (Bellingham, WA: Logos Bible Software, 2015).
2. This point, among others in this list, has been adapted from Keith Getty and David Robertson, "10 Reasons Your Church Should Sing Psalms" the *Gospel Coalition* (Blog), February 22, 2019. https://www.thegospelcoalition.org/article/10-reasons-your-church-sing-psalms/.
3. "The psalms cover the whole range of human experiences," Henry Neil Wallace, *Words to God, Word from God: The Psalms in the Prayer and Preaching of the Church* (New York: Routledge, 2005), 144.

58 of them in 24 verses. God gave us psalms that never repeat and others that say the same thing 26 times (Psalms 2; 136). Some psalms explode with emotion, while others are more doctrinal (Psalms 150; 111). They give us words for rejoicing and reflecting (Psalms 47; 23). They tell us there's a time to praise and a time to lament (Psalms 96; 38).[4]

The Psalms equip us to experience the blessed life in every circumstance, through hardship, adversity, loss, lamentation, and complaint. They paint pictures of even hard realities. Psalms shows us why we need to sing about those hard realities.

The Psalms are designed to mature a Christian and a whole congregation in everything they face. They assist God's people to both rejoice and lament their way into the blessedness of life with God in a fallen world. As Scott Aniol has said, "God intends these songs to shape and form who we are as his people."[5]

The Psalms help us to praise God in the face of our enemies. Emphasis on praise does not appear until the very end of this Book of Praises.[6] Aniol notes, ". . . the book actually starts pretty dark, and that darkness continues, with

4. Bob Kauflin, "What Should We Sing? How to Identify a Good Worship Song," DesiringGod.com, April 18, 2024. https://www.desiringgod.org/articles/what-should-we-sing. Accessed July 15, 2025.

5. Scott Aniol, *Musing on God's Music: Forming Hearts of Praise with the Psalms* (Douglasville, GA: G3 Press, 2023), 14.

6. Scott Aniol, *Musing on God's Music*, 12.

occasional glimpses of light, through much of the first 100 psalms."[7]

It's no accident that the first word in the Psalms is "blessed" (Ps. 1:1). The Psalms are written to lead the child of God into the happinesses of the kingdom of God—in spite of the trials and tribulations of life.

We don't need just some of the Psalms—we need all of them if we're to be fully equipped as Christians.

In the words of Scott Aniol:

> *We need the songs of lament; we need the penitential psalms; and we need the psalms of trust, and the wisdom psalms, and litanies, and the psalms of praise. We need them all to form within us a true and proper and realistic imagination of what a truly blessed life in this world happily submitting to the gracious rule of God will be like.*[8]

Sing the Psalms!

Questions

1. What is the best hymnal ever written?
2. What are key reasons why we should sing the Psalms?

Recommended Hymn: "Lord, from Sorrows Deep I Call"

7. Scott Aniol, "Praise in the Midst of Wickedness," *Religious Affections Ministries* (blog), August 26, 2020. *By the Waters of Babylon* (blog), May 29, 2024. https://religiousaffections.org/articles/biblical-studies/praise-in-the-midst-of-wickedness/. Accessed December 23, 2025.

8. Scott Aniol, *Musing on God's Music*, 224.

CHAPTER 28

TEACH YOUR CHILDREN TO SING

Most children won't sing in church when they are young—that is, unless parents intervene. Often parents don't intervene because they are afraid of offending their children or pushing them into something they don't want to do, or they think their children will just pick it up eventually. This is an unfortunate oversight. It is an unprofitable timidity. This means that your "child left to himself" might not sing for a long time (Prov. 29:15). And he'll think it's just fine to do his own thing—even in church.

A Few Tips

First, make it plain that, when the family goes to church, we go to sing. We don't sing because we feel like it; we sing because it is the right thing to do. It is not optional. It is the right thing to do because God commands singing in church. Make sure your children understand that singing is a simple matter of obedience to God. He is God, and He has our best interests in mind.

Second, don't let your children mumble their way through the songs. Prevent this by teaching them the techniques of singing. While there are many techniques to improve singing, here is one of the simplest basics: teach your children to open their mouths wide to project their voices. No whispering. No mumbling.

Third, show them proper posture—sitting up straight. "Stand like a singer." This assists in singing properly and also facilitates respect for the sacredness of singing. Corporate worship isn't a time to slouch. Further, standing helps to project the sound. I like the way Ryanne J. Molinari explains this:

> *You are called to sing, so you might as well stand like a singer. Roll your shoulders back, untangle your arms and plant your feet hip-width apart—but keep your knees loose!*[1]

Fourth, when they are little, remind your children to sing when they forget to sing. Help them get back on track.

Fifth, when they are young and don't understand all the words or can't pronounce them, show them that it is really good to simply hum the tune. Words are not necessary at that time.[2] Eventually they will pick up the words—and it will happen very quickly. But don't fall into the trap of thinking that they don't need to sing because they don't understand all the words.

Sixth, make it fun and sing the same songs at home or in the car. Helping them learn the lyrics of the songs will come back to bless them for many years.

---

1. Ryanne J. Molinari, "How Can I Make the Most of the Musical Worship If I'm Not Musical?" 9marks.org, November 19, 2025, https://www.9marks.org/article/how-can-i-make-the-most-of-musical-worship-if-im-not-musical/.

2. Keith & Kristyn Getty, *Sing!*, p. 64.

Our friend Chelsea Nastase has some helpful tips for teaching children to sing:

> *Our children learn what we do, so realize that good singing habits are caught more than taught. Sing during family worship; in the car, spontaneously in your home; greet the day with a song; have zero tolerance for mocking of anyone's voice. [See the Appendix in this book for lots more detail.]*

Christian parents have a responsibility to sing and to teach their kids to sing. This starts at home, not at church. This culture is best built from the ground up, starting with the littlest ones. It means that the whole church should be instructed from the Word of God on the importance of singing. This means that you will hear the sounds of children's voices—a sign that these songs will carry them wherever they go—and the words of "Jesus Shall Reign" will be fulfilled among you:

> *People and realms of every tongue*
> *Dwell on his love with sweetest song,*
> *And infant voices shall proclaim*
> *Their early blessings on his name.*

Teach your children to sing.

Questions

1. Why do most young children fail to sing in church?
2. What's the chief reason we should instruct our children to sing, and what are some practical tips to help them in this pursuit?

Recommended Hymn: "Jesus Shall Reign"

FINAL WORDS

Singing is a signature activity in God's kingdom. Creation was celebrated in song by the angels, and the people of God have been singing since history began. Finally, millions of the redeemed in heaven are singing even now with unquenchable joy. Singing is embedded in the cosmos.

Singing is a wonderful gift. A treasure. Let us cherish it, engage in it, and delight in this beautiful gift from God.

APPENDIX

TEACHING YOUNG CHILDREN TO SING

by Chelsea Nastase

Much of the following is comprised of simple observations I've made over time or things I've found helpful as a music teacher and now a mother of young children. I hope you find some of it helpful! None of this is law!

1. Like anything else we hope to teach our children, what we model for them matters. Often the dispositions our children develop are caught more than they are taught, and I believe this is the case with singing as well. If the home is a place where music and singing are the norm and where there is a culture of joy and singing, children will find it more natural to engage in singing during family worship and corporate worship alike. Modeling a love for singing and a willingness to obey the Lord's command to sing is imperative to teaching children to do the same!
2. The primary place for instructing children how to sing is during daily family worship! Just as we use that time

to teach children how to sit still and pay attention to the Word of God as well as how to pray, family worship also provides a precious opportunity for parents to help their children learn to sing. It's entirely appropriate to insist that children who know how to sing choose to sing during family worship, and this will be much more easily accomplished if there is already a culture of singing established in the home *outside* of family worship time!

3. Singing is definitely commanded in Scripture, and I don't think you should back off that point at all! It might also be worth balancing that with the words in James that say: "Is anyone cheerful? Let him sing praise" (James 5:13 ESV). My pastor often says that singing ought to be the natural outlet for our praise to God. We ought to be so full of praise to our Lord that it overflows in song! Again, when this is true in the hearts of believing parents, it should come out in song, and it should shape that culture of joyful song in the home.

4. Some practical tips for establishing a culture of singing in the home might be:
    - Greeting your children with a song in the morning: for young children, that might mean opening their bedroom door and singing to them as you walk in to help them start their day, or singing to and with them while you change their diapers and help them get dressed.
    - Sing spontaneously throughout the day! This doesn't have to be long or formal. Frequency matters more than length!
    - Singing or humming during daily household activities: we often sing while doing daily household chores like

sweeping or doing the dishes. I've found that cleaning up the kitchen after lunch is a great time for me to teach or review hymns with my children since they're still in their highchairs finishing their lunch and are a captive audience. It's amazing how many words they can pick up through informal instruction!

- Having doctrinally solid, artistically beautiful music playing in the home throughout the day: I find this particularly beneficial for my own spiritual wellbeing, and it helps bring truth to mind in the midst of busy days with littles! But beyond that, it also familiarizes children with good music, fills their minds and hearts with Scriptural truths, and implicitly teaches that music is something that's valued in the home.
- Not shying away from singing, even if you're self-conscious about it at first: the more you sing, the more your children will sing. The more expressively you sing, the more expressively your children will sing. The more you enjoy singing, the more your children will enjoy singing. You are their primary, God-given instructor in all things, including the area of joyful singing!
- Having zero tolerance for any mocking of anyone's voice. Even a glimpse of this sort of attitude or behavior discourages children from singing.
- Encouraging your children when you hear them singing, even if they're not yet singing in tune or don't know all the words. Praise the effort, and encourage them that when they sing, they're obeying God! Encourage them that it's wonderful for praise to proceed "out of the mouths of babies and infants" (Ps. 8:2 ESV).

5. Some ideas for teaching youngsters to sing hymns and spiritual songs might include:
   - Some families find it helpful to home in on one or two songs a week (ideally songs that will be sung on the following Lord's Day) and sing these songs daily during family worship time to familiarize their children with the words and melody. For young children, singing a song with a repetitive portion (like a chorus or refrain) might be helpful.
   - I've also found it helpful to pick one hymn to focus on and spend a week (or more, if it takes longer!) on just one verse. I make up motions to help them remember the words, and then I can engage even the youngest child who can barely talk. (On a side note, this works wonderfully well for helping young children memorize Scripture or catechism questions as well!) When they learn one verse, we move to the next verse, and we continue until the hymn is memorized. In terms of when to do this, I do it outside of our evening family worship time. In the mornings, while my husband works, I take fifteen minutes to read and discuss a short Bible story with my children, work on some Scripture memory or catechism questions, and practice whatever hymn we're working on. It's amazing to see how many hymns and songs young children can memorize in this manner!
   - Make a playlist of songs that are frequently sung at your church. Play this playlist often in your home! One day when you're singing together in the car or in the home, your child will surprise you by beginning to sing along!

6. Some practical tips on singing technique:
    - Stand or sit tall but relaxed. Roll your shoulders back. Imagine there's a string coming out of the crown of your head, like a marionette puppet, and someone is pulling it straight. There aren't any strings on your shoulders (your shoulders should be nice and relaxed with no tension); the string is only coming out of the crown of your head. If you're sitting, keep your feet flat on the floor and your back tall. If you're standing, keep your feet shoulder-width apart and firmly planted. Whether standing or sitting, keep your hips, shoulders, and head in a tall, straight line—a relaxed line, not a tense one!
    - Relax your face, neck, jaw, and shoulders. Singing shouldn't be tense or strained. The more you can eliminate tension and keep a relaxed, tall posture, the easier you will find it to sing!
    - Take deep breaths. Send the air down, deep into the bottom of your lungs. Feel your stomach, back, and sides expand as you inhale. Keep your shoulders relaxed. If your shoulders rise while taking a breath, that's a signal that the breath is a shallow breath instead of a deep one.
    - Smile! You will truly enjoy singing more if you do it with a smile on your face.
7. A few various tips and thoughts:
    - Children tend either to mumble or shout while singing. Neither is ideal! When encouraging children to sing, I like to ask them to sing "strongly" or "with gusto" while still encouraging a "pleasant tone." Young children should be singing in their "head voice" (the light, high, "kid" voice), not their "chest voice" (a belting voice that most recorded, adult singers use). Children's tender voices need time

to grow and gain strength before they're really able to belt without hurting their vocal folds (vocal cords). For this reason, I try to avoid words like "loud" since I've found this encourages shouting or belting and does more harm than good to both children's voices and the quality of the sound they're able to produce while singing. Instead, I encourage techniques such as good posture, deep breaths or diaphragmatic breathing, opening the mouth wider and enunciating the words in order to let more sound out, and proper vowel formation. These techniques allow more of that "pleasant tone" or head voice without compromising children's voices.

- Children have a limited vocal range (C4 through E5, or middle C to the E that's nine white keys higher than middle C on a piano). Most hymn melodies are written in musical keys that fit within that range. When possible, play the first pitch of the song on an instrument or pitch pipe before beginning to ensure that the hymn is sung in a range that children can actually sing.

Made in the USA
Coppell, TX
15 June 2026

81682481R00085